OWNING
TOMORROW

THE UNSTOPPABLE FORCE OF DISRUPTIVE LEADERSHIP

JOHN
FREDERICK
FURTH

INDIE BOOKS
INTERNATIONAL

ISBN-10: 1-947480-22-7

ISBN-13: 978-1-947480-22-3

Library of Congress Control Number: 2018942828

PRAISE FOR *OWNING TOMORROW*

"In an age of constant disruption, John Furth has identified and codified a powerful roadmap to inciting and managing change. Owning Tomorrow *provides the kind of pragmatic and logical advice leaders committed to not only creating but actively transforming the future should heed."*
Tristan Louis, President and CEO, Casebook PBC

"Until I read Owning Tomorrow, *I had only a vague understanding of how powerful disruptive leadership can be. However, John's insights, inspiring stories, and practical tools illustrated how valuable disruption can be. It renewed my energy and commitment to helping my family, friends, clients and especially myself achieve goals way beyond what we ever thought possible. I intend to be "Owning Tomorrow" every day."*
Al Zdenek, President & CEO, Traust Solus, Wealth Management

"I found John Furth's book to be full of great insights. Many key learnings I've picked-up throughout my career that has helped me be a better leader is in Owning Tomorrow. *This is a smart book by a smart author for smart people."*
Dana Deasy, former CIO of BP, plc and JPMorgan Chase

"In my coaching sessions with John, I find he has an amazing way of disrupting me and making me think further into the future about my actions and my purpose. Although a book is not always a good substitute for working closely with someone like John, I was amazed how much I learned from reading Owning Tomorrow. *I'm pleased that so many people in the world will now have the opportunity to benefit from John's thinking and approach."*
Ella Rivkin, CEO, ERPS Group

"John Furth has written a fascinating and extremely useful book. Drawing on his extensive personal and professional experiences as a strategist, management consultant, and CEO, he has created a terrific tool for executives with high ambitions to develop themselves and their organizations beyond what they thought possible."

John Connolly, President & CEO, Castle Connolly Medical Ltd. and publisher of America's Top Doctors

"As a business leader I am committed to disrupting industries which have failed to keep pace with consumers needs and are no longer providing them with the kinds of goods, services, and experiences that they want and need. I was therefore very excited to read John Furth's new book Owning Tomorrow. *Furth not only understands the enormity of the challenges—and opportunities—of disrupting entrenched systems but he also offers a wealth of insights, stories, and suggestions to everyone who aspires to become the best business disruptor and leader possible."*

Paul Massara, Board Member, Electron; formerly CEO of RWE Npower and Executive Committee Member of Centrica Plc

*"*Owning Tomorrow, *immediately became my internal compass for my personal and business True North. I found that reading the book gave me a much needed framework and helped organize my thinking around things that John and I have discussed at length. I suspect I'll be re-reading it a lot in the future."*

Inga Romanoff, CEO, Romanoff Consultants

"These are challenging times to be a leader. Whether you own a business, just started a budding tech start-up or are a seasoned executive at a large corporation, you need to do the right things today to stay on top in tomorrow's business world. In his book Owning Tomorrow *John Furth eloquently makes the case that the best way to do that is to master disruptive management practices. John lays out a very methodical process of how to become the best disruptive leader you can be.* Owning Tomorrow *resonated with me tremendously. I couldn't put it down."*

Dirk Schwarz, Chief Revenue Officer, T+ink

TABLE OF CONTENTS

PREFACE

WE'RE LIVING IN THE AGE OF DISRUPTION

For most of the world's population, December 31, 1999, wasn't that much different than any other New Year's Eve. Like hundreds of thousands of New Yorkers, I had been invited to a small dinner party. At 11:45 p.m., my hosts, fellow guests, and I donned our year 2000 spectacles, grabbed noisemakers, confetti and a glass of champagne, and headed to the roof deck to watch fireworks over Manhattan.

The only potentially extraordinary event was the collapse of the world's computer systems the minute the clocks turned to 12:00 a.m. on January 1, 2000—the so-called Y2K bug (decades earlier somebody had forgotten to put enough zeros in a key piece of software code.) But that frisson of anticipation disappeared quickly. Y2K turned out to be a nonevent.

During the early days of the new millennium, I doubt there was anyone on Earth who could have predicted the series of disruptive events that would unfold during the next few years. Coming at a fast pace, many of these incidents were highly destructive. But a handful of global events supported and accelerated positive developments of many of the world's most established and powerful educational, religious, governmental, and business institutions.

For the first time since World War II, the United States was attacked on its own soil when a handful of Islamic terrorists flew airplanes into key buildings in New York City and Washington, DC, on September 11, 2001, killing over 3,000 American citizens. Routine cyberattacks on our information technology (IT) systems have made the potential Y2K meltdown look like child's play. Rival powers such as China have stolen vast stores of intellectual property while Russia blatantly meddled in our electoral process.

The financial correction of 2001 may not have been such a surprise to many experts, but even the smartest among us were blindsided by the crisis of 2007-2008. We are still feeling the disruptive effects of the near-collapse of the world's financial system.

As of 1999, Amazon's revenue had only just passed the billion-dollar mark, and if anyone used the term "social media," they were probably referring to how TV, newspapers, and magazines covered parties thrown by the rich and famous. Seventeen years later, Amazon is fast approaching $200 billion in revenue and over two billion people use some form of social media; ninety percent have a Facebook account.

Mark Zuckerberg, the founder and CEO of Facebook, became the youngest self-made billionaire at twenty-seven when the company went public in 2012. Like Bill Gates before him, he proved that completing a college degree at Harvard isn't necessarily a prerequisite for success, happiness, and wealth.

But a Chinese conglomerate, Alibaba, is currently the largest company in the world. And despite its size, Alibaba is growing much faster than its main competitor, Amazon, a company that has successfully used disruptive tools and techniques to quickly build a large, sustainable global organization.

Despite its negative connotations, the word "disruption" has become part of our *lingua franca*. When businesspeople talk about disruptive technologies, disruptive innovation, and disruptive business models, they are often referring to management practices that have the power to transform individuals, companies, and indeed large portions of society while generating huge value for thousands (if not millions) of people.

These days, the most ambitious millennials aspire to become disruptive leaders and not just mere entrepreneurs or CEOs. Many older leaders also understand that if they aren't prepared to actively disrupt how they run their businesses, the expiration date on their careers and companies will come sooner than expected. The truly great ones not only proactively disrupt themselves but also their employees, their investors, their families, and even their competitors in their burning desire to make an impact and create unimaginable wealth.

Unfortunately, I've witnessed leaders stuck in situations that just keep getting worse, going from disaster to disaster, where entrenched thinking prevails, and where leadership avoids disruption at any cost. Employees, suppliers, customers, and investors lose faith but keep soldiering on, hoping things will improve until the day someone has the guts to call it a failure and everybody feels even worse than before.

But I've also had the good fortune of meeting and working with a few well-known, disruptive CEOs. In addition, I spent almost two years interviewing and researching other famous and not-so-famous disruptors for this book. While some of the men and women I profile in these pages lead multinational companies, many own and/or run small and medium-size organizations.

Owning Tomorrow: The Unstoppable Force of Disruptive Leadership is intended to help senior executives and leaders with ambitions to develop themselves and their organizations beyond what they thought was possible. Even though so much is changing in the twenty-first century, many existing best practices in business such as good decision-making, maintaining healthy cash flow, and building a values-driven organization are the same for disruptive companies as they are for any well-functioning enterprise. If those are missing, no company—disruptive or otherwise—can last very long.

But this is not just a book for the upper echelons of management. It is for anyone interested in creating a future of abundant success and fulfillment. Never give up on your future no matter what life throws at you. As long as you embrace the unstoppable force of disruption and develop the right skills and mindset you will live a life of abundance, success and happiness; but more importantly, no one will own your tomorrow except you.

John Furth
May 2018

At the end of several parts of *Owning Tomorrow* you'll be guided to free materials relevant to that part. These can be found at **www.JohnFFurth. com/diagnostics** or **www.JohnFFurth.com/ worksheets** and include tools, templates, and an assessment you can download and use as well as an online survey that assesses your disruptive leadership style and capabilities.

PART ONE

DISRUPTION IS NOT FOR THE FAINT OF HEART

SECTION 1

The Transformative Power of Business Disruption

Thousands of years ago, human beings discovered the best way to increase our standard of living was to create order out of chaos by constantly inventing and reinventing our most important tools: technology, processes, and systems.

Universities, businesses, and governments became the primary agencies for developing and promoting advances in these tools. These could then be combined in a multitude of ways to constantly improve the human condition. Currency was developed and accepted as a global standard for trading goods, precisely because it provided humankind with a better and more reliable system to value goods and services than bartering.

Evolving processes and systems have made it easier, faster, and cheaper to get food, clothing, and other goods and services we need. They have enabled us to make education available to billions of people, travel almost anywhere in the world more quickly and inexpensively, be entertained 24/7, treat diseases more efficiently and effectively, and on and on.

The problem is, as soon as we've gotten used to a system, it often becomes a target for yet another improvement. We suddenly find our lives disrupted, plunged temporarily back into chaos as we adjust to a new way of doing things. And despite the longer-term benefits to humanity, almost every meaningful large-scale disruption produces winners and losers in the short run.

No wonder, then, that most people still associate disruption with upheaval, starvation, and death, and not with renewal, reinvention, and rebirth. Even a great thinker like Clayton Christensen of Harvard Business School tells us that although technological and business model

3

disruptions have led to profound innovations that have improved mankind's standard of living, they have also hurt successful well-managed companies. To some degree, the disruption of many traditional American businesses has laid waste to rust-belt communities while contributing in no small way to the great recession and rising income inequality. And as technology advances at lightning speed, all of this is happening faster and faster.

Entrepreneurs are usually the ones who bring about the most impactful and transformative disruptions. The most ambitious among them often also see disruption as the best way to build a significant company in a short amount of time. Despite the long-term positive advances, however, these disruptions can also generate short-term losers, often in the form of bankrupt companies, unemployed workers, and/or widespread economic uncertainty.

On the other hand, established organizations and leaders generally use disruptive techniques to swiftly and powerfully turn around a quickly deteriorating situation. Frequently, this kind of disruption is about reversing a collective mindset or a generally agreed-to way of doing things, which can be even more difficult in some cases than simply starting greenfield with a disruptive idea. The impetus for such disruptions is less about a radically new vision for affecting the human condition and more about saving an organization in trouble.

Powerful disruptions at first can appear counterintuitive, irrational, and unreasonable precisely because most disruptions bear little resemblance to the past and actively go against prevailing beliefs about what's right. For this reason—and because they can appear destructive at first, especially if longer-term benefits are not clear—powerful disruptions are often accompanied by widespread controversy, confusion, and derision.

The wide adoption of the internet for commerce, communication, information, and entertainment starting in the early 1990s coincided with the first academic explorations of disruption. These new technologies enabled entrepreneurs to build companies without huge initial investments that had previously been needed for buildings, infrastructure, and legions of employees. Disruption became easier—and cheaper—to do.

In addition to Clay Christensen, professors like Luke Williams and Michael Raynor have laid the groundwork to help us better understand the power of disruption. Businessmen and entrepreneurs such as Lou Gerstner of IBM, Michael Dell, Reed Hastings of Netflix, and Jeff Bezos of Amazon have proven how successful disruptions can generate enormous value, not only for a company's shareholders but also for billions of consumers and customers around the world. Disruptive leadership and the right processes can accelerate growth, performance, effectiveness, and success for executives and their businesses, regardless of size, industry segment and location. Disruptive methodologies are also proving to be faster and more powerful than many prevailing methodologies, such as business transformation, change management, etc., especially for small and medium-size businesses.

Amazon: The Company That Decides Who Gets Disrupted and When

P robably no other organization in the world better embodies the power of audacious and continual disruption than Amazon. This is the company which, upon its founding by Bezos in 1994, took on small and large booksellers around the world. Along the way, it forced many incumbents to disrupt their business models or turn off the lights.

The short-term negative consequences of the actions of Bezos and his team, however, were overshadowed by the immense value they created providing billions of books and other printed material to people around the world more efficiently and cheaply than previously possible. The stock market rewarded Amazon with an almost 5,000 percent increase in its stock price within two years of the company going public in 1997.

Amazon also disrupted the then-prevailing system that required consumers to do exhaustive research, read book reviews, talk to friends, and visit libraries and book stores before buying a book. Other consumers simply bought books based on titles and descriptions on jacket covers. Both approaches—and others—were at best inefficient and often ended in disappointment for the purchasers.

Jeff Bezos and his team changed those systems dramatically by pioneering cutting-edge algorithms that could pinpoint individual consumer desires—or at least make informed recommendations—sometimes even before the customer was aware of them. By the mid-1990s consumers could research and order books 24/7 and receive them whenever and wherever they wanted, with high assurance that the product would be what they expected it to be.

As Amazon gained the trust of consumers around the world, the company was able to leverage those relationships to challenge the entrenched major publishing houses and their traditional business and operating models. Amazon disrupted and changed the economics of publishing and made it easy and inexpensive for young and first-time authors to publish and sell books that the traditional publishing world often ignored. Less well-known writers were given the opportunity to tap into a huge, international market of potential readers which had theretofore been unavailable to them.

Jeff Bezos and his team then went on to dominate a few segments of a completely different industry: consumer electronics. They successfully disrupted Sony, Apple, and Samsung's early domination of two large categories: e-readers (Barnes & Noble only comes in a distant fifth with the Nook) and tablets.

Amazon even created an entirely new category of voice-activated smart speakers with its Amazon Echo. By applying its formidable logistics capabilities and algorithms to other e-commerce segments such as perishable goods, clothing, toys, and so on, the company quickly became the second-largest online retailer in the world. By the end of 2016, it was clear the company had plans to disrupt and transform the brick-and-mortar grocery industry, initially announcing its first small-format grocery store, Amazon Go, then acquiring Whole Foods six months later.

Even in markets such as video streaming services and original movie and TV content, where they were later to the game than other companies, Amazon has grabbed significant market and mindshare. In just a few seasons the company has produced major, critically acclaimed shows like *The Man in the High Castle*, *Transparent*, and *The Marvelous Mrs. Maisel*.

There are a few companies that have been able to successfully disrupt at best one or two industry segments (Microsoft, for example, managed to change the face of the computing and the video gaming industries). But Amazon is the only company in recent history that has successfully disrupted at least four or five completely different industries or market segments.

But what exactly is it that has kept Amazon at the height of its powers for almost twenty-five years?

Amazon is not only capable of disrupting companies and even entire industries, the company has proven over and over again that it is also able to disrupt and transform itself. Amazon constantly updates and refines (i.e., disrupts) its logistics, fulfillment, and management systems to stay ahead of its competitors' and customers' demands, even if the customer doesn't explicitly ask for it.

What exactly is it that has kept Amazon at the height of its powers for almost twenty-five years?

For one, Amazon is willing to fight to succeed, occasionally resorting to aggressive, no-holds-barred tactics. The company has a culture that is innovative and pioneering. They can hire the best and brightest technology experts, engineers, lawyers, and businesspeople in the world to make things happen.

The answer is much simpler, but also more profound. At the heart of everything Amazon does is a short but powerful mission statement: "Our vision is to be Earth's most customer-centric company; to build a place where people can come to find and discover anything they might want to buy online."

In contrast, Apple has a relatively exhaustive and exhausting mission statement: "Apple designs Macs, the best personal computers in the world, along with OS X, iLife, iWork and professional software. Apple leads the digital music revolution with its iPods and iTunes online store. Apple has reinvented the mobile phone with its revolutionary iPhone and App store, and is defining the future of mobile media and computing devices with iPad."

Or consider that of Barnes & Noble, Amazon's only remaining competitor in the book market, which states their mission is "to operate the *best* omni-channel specialty retail business in America, helping both our customers and booksellers reach their aspirations while being a credit to the communities we serve."

Netflix's mission is "to grow our streaming subscription business domestically and globally. We are continuously improving the customer experience, with a focus on expanding our streaming content, enhancing our user interface and extending our streaming service to even more Internet-connected devices, while staying within the parameters of our consolidated net income and operating segment contribution profit targets."

Only two other large internet companies come close to capturing Amazon's powerful and highly customer-centric mission. One is the global e-commerce platform eBay, whose mission is "to be the world's favorite destination for discovering great value and unique selection." The other is Facebook. Its mission is to "give people the power to build community and bring the world closer together."

The fact is, most companies focus on *what they do* and/or what great widgets they have *created* or *own*, and *not what they are*. This is true whether they are big or small, high-tech or low tech, business-to-consumer (B2C) or business-to-business (B2B) companies. The problem is that technologies, business models, and products can be disrupted and challenged at the drop of a hat. Systems, tools, processes, etc. are meant to be discarded, changed, or updated in our never-ending quest for something better.

Because Amazon's entire reason for being is to provide its customers with the highest possible value, the company is not hampered by proprietary technology, products, or systems core to its mission which could easily be made redundant by even more forward-thinking and aggressive competitors. Bezos and his team have no interest in maintaining any technology or system that doesn't contribute to making Amazon the most customer-centric company in the world.

The company's unique mission is reinforced by fourteen principles into which every leader is indoctrinated through training and development. These principles inform all key strategic choices or decisions. Products and services are stress-tested to ensure they are in line with these values as well as to the mission. The company's hiring, promotion, and retention processes are designed to ensure that prospective and current employees understand and live the organization's mission to the greatest extent possible.

But even the best-run companies are far from perfect, and Amazon is no exception. A lot gets lost in the cracks of its global operations, and there are legions of vendors who have gone bust or have lost a lot of money selling through Amazon.

A case in point is the company my friend Benjamin works for. He is part of a team that manages a portfolio of mid-priced and luxury branded consumer jewelry and watches. One afternoon in the summer of 2017, he told me the story of how their sales on Amazon went from boom to nearly bust and back to boom again as they tried to navigate a vendor program that turned out to be less-than-advantageous for them.

In the early 2000s Benjamin's company was successfully part of Amazon's seller platform. Growth was so explosive that by mid-2007 Amazon approached the company to become part of a new vendor program. Benjamin hadn't joined the company yet, but his colleagues were told that the Amazon vendor program was an exclusive, invite-only affair, something that appealed to brands with a certain cachet of exclusivity.

The vendor program offered some compelling features, such as a full-time service person assigned to the company's account, active promotion programs that would introduce its products to top reviewers before they ever hit the shelves, and extended versions of basic product descriptions.

With few competitors and stable pricing, sales of the company's products on the new vendor program initially grew very quickly. But at the time, the team didn't understand just how much these programs would cost while failing to deliver a lot of what had been promised.

For example, the service person assigned to Benjamin's company cost $280,000 per year. This wouldn't have been so terrible had that person been more active, but she was constantly in training programs and not available when the organization needed her, even though she was presumably working exclusively on its behalf.

On top of this, Benjamin's company was paying 10 percent of all sales to promote its products, plus freight allowances and damage allowances. All in all, at least 45 percent of the retail price was going straight to Amazon. The company was also pressured into using the Amazon Media group (AMG) for advertising. All charges were billed immediately to the vendor account, yet receipts were delayed by 180 days, making cash-flow forecasting problematic.

To add insult to injury, Amazon was cutting the product's prices—a huge danger for any brand that counts on being premium-priced across all channels.

Benjamin's biggest disappointment was with what Amazon calls FBA—"fulfillment by Amazon." On the surface, it appeared to be a good deal. Amazon would take over all delivery service once it received the products. But Benjamin discovered that about 20 percent of their products were being returned to Amazon's warehouses damaged. Amazon did little or no quality check (despite assurances to the contrary) and these damaged goods would be then sent to new customers without informing the company. The resulting confusion, disappointment, and brand erosion among their consumers were significant.

Amazon had also sold the company on a sophisticated forecasting tool that would help them send the right number of items to Amazon's fulfillment centers at the appropriate time. What Benjamin later discovered was that this forecasting model was only reliable when categories were aggregated at the highest level, such as menswear or womenswear, but the information on watches and jewelry wasn't accurate at all. As a result, the flow of product was not optimized, and Amazon assessed storage fees if products sat on the shelves too long or unsold product was sent back.

This was the straw that broke the camel's back, and because there was no ombudsman to complain to, Benjamin and his team went directly to management. They dug into the faulty forecasting model and finally got Amazon to agree that it was not working. Eventually, the terms of their agreement was renegotiated. Today, Benjamin's products are selling briskly again, and he expects about a 400 percent increase in sales during the first year of the new agreement.

Despite this and other problems with vendors and customers, Amazon is by any measure a huge success. The company's impact is not just limited to its internal and external stakeholders. Having seen the benefits of the Amazon model in their daily lives, many business customers now bring data, preferences, and analytics to the table when purchasing supplies for their businesses. B2B companies have jettisoned traditional catalog-based ordering systems, preferring to offer real-time interaction, extensive price/inventory transparency, and robust guided selling.

In the process, leaders of B2B companies have had to also disrupt most of their basic beliefs about business and competition. The marketplace is becoming far more crowded, with start-ups and pop-ups competing against established businesses, and a high degree of expansion of existing suppliers, such as Staples, into niche markets, such as medical devices.

Commerce has become frictionless. This means transactions become as easy as possible. Studies have shown that every additional step required for checkout reduces online sales revenue by 30 percent; for omni-channel commerce, frictionless purchasing may mean enabling a customer to transact among channels, such as relocating a movie from a computer or television screen to a phone or tablet screen. Frictionless commerce can also exist between products, allowing a customer to upgrade easily from a freemium to a paid service, or from a basic add-on service to an upsold premium service.

At the same time that Amazon was going from success to success, a company that had risen quickly to become the mightiest player in the consumer electronics and entertainment industries was about to be disrupted within an inch of its life. That company was Sony.

SECTION 3

Beware the Danger of Nondisruption

From its start in 1946, Sony went against all prevailing beliefs about the electronics industry. The company was an upstart in postwar Japan, a country which until then had not been thought of as a hub of innovation for electronics. Companies in the United States and Germany were the market leaders, and it was inconceivable that businesses from other countries could make a considerable dent in their domination of the industry.

So, Sony's executives did the only thing they could do under the circumstances—they blatantly stole ideas and technology from the West, improved on them, and made them their own with great success.

By the time the company's most famous product, the Sony Walkman, arrived on the scene in the 1980s, Sony was clearly the world leader in most segments of the consumer electronics industry. (Interestingly, few people at the time noted publicly that the Walkman wasn't much more than a stereo version of a transistor radio with a cassette player added in for good measure.)

But with the death of Sony's founder and visionary, Akio Morita, and the creeping Japanese malaise of the "social contract" between employees and employers, Sony handed its leadership over to companies more openly disruptive, such as Canon, Apple, Samsung, and LG. By the beginning of the new millennium, these competitors had taken market share away from Sony in a few key product categories such as cameras and TVs. Some competitors—including IBM and Amazon—had even created new segments that the decision-makers at Sony were unable to develop the right products for, such as electronic readers and tablets.

This is not to imply that Sony's engineers were not excellent at what they did. But the engineering values they had previously cherished and which had made Sony successful for decades, such as quality, excellent design, longevity, and fidelity were no longer relevant in the marketplace. Other values, such as sharing (as in the case of MP3s), agility, and ease of use had replaced them.

Sony was still widely considered to be the most powerful company in the consumer electronics and entertainment industries when I moved to Tokyo, Japan in 2003 to work as the chief strategist in the CEO's Office for Strategy. Internally, however, it was clear to most executives that Sony was losing ground fast and the CEO who had hired me, Nobuyuki Idei, was being held accountable for the deteriorating situation. In one of those contradictory moves that are so common at Japanese corporations, Sony's leadership asked my team—all of whom had been chosen by Idei—to think about the options for a replacement CEO who could turn the situation around.

There was only one senior executive in Japan with the credibility and leadership skills to succeed at such a difficult undertaking. That person was Ken Kutaragi, a brilliant, no-holds-barred businessman. He had built the Sony PlayStation from scratch into the category-defining product it had become by 2005. This was before Xbox spent billions of dollars to push it off its pedestal.

But Kutaragi was deemed "too disruptive," and Sony's board was afraid he would polarize the organization—which, in hindsight, was most likely exactly what Sony needed.

At the time, Japan was all abuzz about the positive effects Carlos Ghosn was having at Nissan as the first foreign-born CEO of a major Japanese corporation. Thus, my team and I decided the next best option was to help Sony's leadership understand the benefits and risks of hiring an "outsider" to run the company. In my presentations to Sony senior executives, I continually brought up the work Gerstner had done at IBM as an example of positive changes that could happen when an experienced noncompany man was brought in as a force of change. To support my argument, at one point I even facilitated a few meetings between Lou Gerstner, IBM's CEO in the 1990s who successfully disrupted and turned the company around, his successor at IBM Sam Palmisano, and Mr. Idei.

Unfortunately, behind closed doors—and sometimes to my face—many middle managers and directors dismissed these ideas out of hand. Sony was primarily a B2C business and not a B2B IT house like IBM, they said. The comparison to a car company was considered even more ridiculous. Most of these colleagues saw virtually no similarities between Nissan and a consumer electronics and entertainment company like Sony.

But this characterization of Sony was a little misleading. Like many Japanese conglomerates, the company dabbled in hundreds of unrelated activities, such as cosmetics and pharmaceuticals. It even owned a restaurant, Maxim's of Paris, simply because cofounder Akio Morita loved the place and wanted to have it. There were also other businesses that were a little closer to Sony's core business such as semiconductors, retail, and medical imaging.

But it didn't matter what leadership thought if thousands of middle-management executives didn't get it. Sony's board faced a dilemma. They knew the organization wasn't going to accept a person who was not Japanese *and* someone who had never worked at Sony before as their new CEO.

Thus, it came as no surprise to me that the final choice to become the company's next CEO was Howard Stringer. At that time, Howard was the successful head of Sony America as well as global president of the company's entertainment divisions worldwide, having taken both divisions through major restructurings in the 2000s. He was also widely liked and respected within the company.

To his credit, Howard was, at least in private conversations with me, not at all convinced he was the right choice to be CEO of the entire company, preferring instead to be seen and employed as a kind of chief restructurer. Howard knew full well that he was a movie and TV guy, not an engineer. That meant he would never truly understand the mainstay of Sony's business, consumer electronics. But that didn't stop him from accepting the position. Ken Kutaragi promptly left the company with more than $100 million he had earned as president of Sony PlayStation.

I briefed Howard several times about who he could count on to be allies in Tokyo headquarters and who he should watch out for. Knowing just how difficult the task would be, Howard and his team developed an if-all-else-fails solution if they couldn't effect the change needed. This plan would have spun off many of the assets into a number of more easily manageable pieces.

My two-year contract at Sony was coming to an end, and I was tired of the daily maneuverings of my Japanese colleagues trying to box me in and keep me out of the loop. (This was no different than how they treated any senior executive in Japan who was a foreigner, given Sony's notoriously engineering driven, inward-facing culture.) I figured I had done as much as I could. I then headed to my next position as the head of international strategy for Discovery International, the TV company headquartered outside of Washington, DC.

From the depth of my heart, I genuinely wished Howard all the best and wanted him to succeed. Despite my own personal issues with being a foreign senior executive at the heart of what was, in the end, still a very Japanese company, I hoped I had helped pave the way for something better and more revolutionary to happen. Unfortunately, not much of any good transpired in the next five years.

There were many things that contributed to Howard's ultimate failure, but two stand out:

1. **Howard was not willing to move his home to Tokyo.** That meant that he would never develop the kind of relationships he needed to have with the engineers and product evangelists who dreamed up and developed the consumer electronics that Sony was known for. (All Sony's consumer products businesses were headquartered in Japan, and even foreign engineers reported to someone in Japan.) By not establishing a home in Japan, he also sent the message that he wasn't going to "slug it through" with the rest of Sony's leadership and the majority of the company's employees.

2. **Howard's low-key and highly diplomatic personality helped him survive Sony's internal politics but cost the company dearly.** He unwittingly perpetuated most of the worst aspects of Sony's culture even though he knew that the inward-looking engineering focus of much of the organization was backward and ill-suited for the needs of a modern consumer electronics company. Any great ideas he had about changing the culture met with silent resistance.

Thus, even though Howard was an "insider," he also remained an "outsider" who was never able to gain the trust and familiarity with the people who might have ultimately helped him push through an aggressive agenda. Worse still, the Japanese saw most of his ideas as hopelessly American and therefore not part of Sony's DNA. Needless to say, with the exception of selling a few of the obviously small and noncore businesses—Maxim's was one of the first to go—Howard's if-all-else-fails solution never saw the light of day.

By the time of Howard's retirement in 2013, Sony's stock had lost 75 percent of its value. Adding to Sony's declining market share in cameras and computers under Mr. Idei, Sony's dominance in other markets, such as broadcast equipment, computer games, cell phones, and computers, eroded measurably during Howard's tenure. The fear of cannibalizing some of the company's most important businesses—despite all the warning signs—meant that Sony was too slow to develop the kind of cutting-edge products and services using internet and digital technologies that had once made Sony great.

The real irony of the story—as I only discovered when writing this book—is that Lou Gerstner advised Howard throughout most of his tenure. Maybe all those middle manager "salary men" in Japan were right after all. What worked for Gerstner at IBM was not transferable to a company like Sony, and it seems his advice was not particularly helpful.

SECTION 4

A Rogues' Gallery of Disruptive Leaders

Leaders tend to fall into one of three categories. While the first group is composed almost exclusively of entrepreneurs, those in the second and third groups are usually experienced leaders and managers.

1. **The Young Leaders.** A handful of men and women in every generation appear to have been born with great leadership instincts, ambition, and intelligence. They often become successes early in their careers. Think of Mark Zuckerberg, Jeff Bezos, and Bill Gates.

2. **The Accidental Leaders.** These are the few souls who suddenly find themselves propelled into positions of leadership regardless of whether they planned or even wanted it. Unfortunately, they often lack or never bother developing certain important skill sets. Sometimes they work hard to fill the gaps, but often they simply fail to deliver on what is expected of them.

   Howard Stringer is a perfect example of an accidental leader.

3. **The Developed Leaders:** This last category still represents the majority of CEOs. These men and women have worked and studied hard and successfully climbed the corporate ladder to achieve positions of leadership. (Lou Gerstner is just one of many good examples.)

Luck and being at the right place at the right time sometimes play roles in a leader's success. But most leaders actively develop and master a variety of skills, especially the ability to disrupt anything that comes between leaders and the growth and sustainability of their organizations.

Good career planning and taking on increasingly demanding positions are the traditional ways in which developed leaders learn and refine their capabilities. But these days not all leaders—especially those who fall into the first two categories—have the luxury of time or opportunity to learn everything they need to know. Education, reading and actively being coached, mentored, and trained has become more important for developing our best leaders.

In fact, I can only think of two God-given natural talents that all successful leaders are born with. Everything else is learned.

The first important natural talent is a high level of intelligence. All the traditional school-based education, books, and life lessons mean little if the ability to process information and other inputs quickly and deeply isn't there. Highly intelligent people generally learn from everything and everyone they come in contact with. Many also get bored easily and find it hard to conform to traditional school-based education. In fact, the two single most recognizable entrepreneurs of the last thirty years both dropped out of Harvard before graduating: Bill Gates and Mark Zuckerberg.

High intelligence is to business leaders what innate talent is to musicians or athletes. You or I might be able to shoot hoops very well without a lot of talent using sheer discipline and hard work. Most professional athletes, however, are gifted from the beginning with prodigious amounts of talent, which they then go on to develop.

Like athletic talent which exhibits itself early in life, high intelligence can be spotted at a relatively young age. Because they were born with the ability to use their intelligence, great leaders generally need less time to learn or adopt new skill sets or capabilities. Their extraordinary intelligence gives them the ability to "think outside the box" and create compelling visions that often appear too abstract to less gifted people. Paradoxically, highly intelligent people are also able to grasp and process concrete but very minute details of any situation equally well.

Our society as a whole is quick to pull down the leaders who don't measure up to our expectations. Many outwardly successful leaders may fall from grace quickly when they turn out to be corrupt or liars. Sometimes they were too quick and aggressive to challenge established rules or laws or got blindsided by unexpected events or a political situation they lost control of. Many fail because their pride, ego, or greed got the better of them. But castigating them as stupid is just naïve and, well, *stupid*. You may not like the decisions or behavior of a particular leader, but it doesn't mean he or she isn't highly intelligent.

The other talent I believe every great leader is born with is ambition. Good leaders are not only ambitious for themselves but also for their employees, their customers, and their families. Great business leaders want to leave behind a legacy and create something that is bigger than they are.

Unfortunately, ambitious leaders are often impatient with those less aspirational or intelligent than they are. Combined with their often restless curiosity, it's easy to understand why many leaders often leave behind a lot of strained or even broken relationships. But by the same token, great leaders also create high levels of loyalty, admiration, and gratitude from the people with whom they work and live.

Not everyone with intelligence and ambition become business leaders, as there are many avenues available to people with those gifts. (Indeed, sometimes the idea of starting a business or leading an organization doesn't occur to very successful men and women until their twenties or thirties.) Even then, if intelligence and ambition aren't properly developed and nurtured, these assets can slowly wither away or turn in on themselves.

Then there are the capabilities that successful business leaders need to consciously and diligently develop. A few may come naturally to some leaders, and a few may not. These include but aren't limited to the ability to work hard, be focused and resilient, think strategically, and develop emotional intelligence.

Contrary to popular belief, today's disruptive leaders aren't the outsiders or rugged individualists that modern American mythology likes to portray. Using the results of a study done in 2014, David Moschella developed a list of the most important IT disruptors over the last fifty years and discovered that all of them were straight Caucasian or Asian men.[1]

The men below were either born in the United States or came here to study. Many of them have advanced degrees and most started their own companies and never worked for anybody but themselves.

Gene Amdahl	Larry Ellison	Elon Musk
Marc Andreessen	Don Estridge	Ray Noorda
Gordon Bell	Boe Evans	Robert Noyce
Marc Benioff	Shawn Fanning	Ken Olsen
Tim Berners-Lee	Janus Friis	Pierre Omidyar
Jeff Bezos	Bill Gates	Ray Ozzie
Leonard Bosack	Andy Grove	Larry Page
Dan Bricklin	Reed Hastings	Ross Perot
Segey Brin	Ted Hoff	Hasso Plattner
Rod Canion	Reid Hoffman	Al Shugart
Steve Case	Steve Jobs	Tom Siebel
Vint Cerf	Bill Joy	Linus Torvalds
Tedd Codd	Mitch Kapor	Jimmy Wales
Scott Cook	Ray Kurzweil	An Wang
Seymour Cray	Mike Lazaridis	Steve Wozniak
Michael Dell	Bob Metcalfe	Mark Zuckerberg
Jack Dorsey	Gordon Moore	

There are a few women CEOs of prominence in the technology industry who could have potentially been on the list, such as Christine Whitman, Carly Fiorina, and Ginny Rometty, but they didn't build and run their own companies. (This is by no means a value judgment. After all, Lou Gerstner—undoubtedly a great disruptor—wasn't an entrepreneur and didn't make the cut, either.)

---

[1] Moschella, David. "50 For 50 – The Most Important IT Disruptors of the Last Half Century." *Leading Edge Forum*, 30 June 2014, leadingedgeforum.com/publication/50-for-50-the-most-important-it-disruptors-of-the-last-half-century-2379/.

In an article based on his findings published by *Leading Edge Forum*, Moschella mentions a few entrepreneurial females of some note in the IT industry such as Judy Estrin, Sandy Lerner, Esther Dyson, and Arianna Huffington. None of them, however, have had the impact of a Jeff Bezos, Steve Jobs, or Bill Gates.

Admittedly, although the list above could also be seen as the who's who of innovative technologists, Moschella calls them "disruptors" because they either went against prevailing beliefs and trends to advance technology or were so creative that they simply revolutionized anything they touched. I consider a few of the men on the list—such as Larry Ellison and Ross Perot—to more be disruptive as personalities than as leaders.

Using my definition of disruption—which includes some sort of negative impact at the beginning which is then overshadowed by vastly greater social and economic good—I would whittle the list down to a few truly disruptive leaders. In addition to Jeff Bezos (on the list) and Lou Gerstner (not on the list), my core group of disruptors would include the following.

- **Michael Dell** radically changed how computers were manufactured and distributed, essentially making his competitors' supply chains obsolete. He forced several large computer manufacturing companies and retailers out of business. Eventually, two of the largest PC companies, Compaq and HP, had to merge to survive. Michael Dell made PCs cheaper, easy to order, and reliable.

- **Reid Hoffman**, the founder of LinkedIn, formed a worldwide marketplace to match companies looking for talent and job seekers, help businesses find clients, and a whole host of value-added activities. In the process, he and his team disintermediated the executive search business and the use of classified ads, among other things. Thirteen years after Hoffman started LinkedIn, at the end of 2016, the company was bought by Microsoft for a whopping $26 billion.

- **Shawn Fanning** basically caused a significant disruption—some would call it destruction—of the music industry with Napster. This early file-sharing program made it relatively easy for music enthusiasts to upload and download copies of songs that were otherwise difficult to obtain, such as older songs, unreleased recordings, and bootleg concert recordings.

- **Reed Hastings** founded Netflix in 1997. After initially renting and selling DVDs, Hastings decided to focus exclusively on the DVD rental-by-mail business. In the process, Netflix put thousands of smaller DVD rental shops out of business. Then Netflix got ahead of itself and starting streaming videos. This strategic error disrupted its own DVD rental model and essentially put *that* business out of business and made Blockbuster a distant memory, although that company still exists as a mere shadow of its former self. But in 2013, with Netflix facing potential bankruptcy, Hastings stunned the world by integrating backward into the production of movies and TV series—and very successfully at that.

Some consider Mark Zuckerberg, the founder of Facebook, to be the poster boy for the new face of business disruption. He is the youngest person in history to achieve a net worth of over $50 billion by starting his own company. Like Bill Gates and Steve Jobs, he also never completed his formal education. Jobs preferred dressing in black turtlenecks and jeans to suits, and Zuckerberg wears his own uniform of a hoody and jeans.

In my view, however, Zuckerberg is more of a genius innovator and entrepreneur who saw an opportunity and went after it aggressively and single-mindedly rather than a disruptor like a Bezos, Dell, or Gates. He and his company also unwittingly provided the platform for a group of Russians to exert immeasurable influence in the 2016 U.S. presidential election which, while highly disruptive, can hardly be described as resulting in a positive and lasting transformation for mankind.

However, what Mark Zuckerberg did disrupt was the world's overriding belief about the amount of time it takes and the age at which someone (albeit a highly capable someone) can become a successful multi-billionaire.

For me, the newer brand of disruptive leadership is represented by Jack Ma, a former eighth-grade teacher in China and founder and CEO of Alibaba, a group of internet-based services. This is the company that raised over $25 billion in an initial public offering on the New York Stock Exchange, making Alibaba the largest IPO in United States financial history. He is also the face of the Chinese industrial juggernaut—possibly the biggest current threat to many American businesses in the twenty-first century.

SECTION 5

Egos and Ethics

Many disruptive leaders not only radically change traditional ways of doing of business but are also committed to challenging generally accepted norms of leadership behavior and business propriety. They are among the most ambitious people in the world and are known to push ethical and legal boundaries in their unrelenting drive to get what they want.

Many of them have learned how to modify their more extreme behaviors when necessary but a few have also gotten so ahead of themselves that their boards had no choice but to fire them.

Travis Kalanick, the former CEO of Uber, is the most recent high-profile example of a successful disruptive leader whose success and ego blinded him to the necessity of building a culture of accountability and ethics and adhere to local and state employment laws. The company was sued, investors left in droves and many municipalities threatened to cancel their licenses.

The descriptions below give us a snapshot of how the world—or at least how the media—views the behavior of several of these leaders.

- "Jeff Bezos may be a visionary, but when it comes to his business, it seems he also has a bit of a murderous streak. He won't let competitors beat him, even if it means killing his core business."[2] *Jill Krasny, technology writer*

- "Jeff may be outwardly goofy, with that trademark laugh, but he's a very tough guy...If he goes even halfway through (any

---

[2] Krasny, Jill. "The Jeff Bezos Recipe for Disruption." Inc.com, *Inc.*, 15 Oct. 2013, www.inc.com/krasny/jeff-bezos-recipe-for-disruption.html.

disruption he undertakes), there is no way he's not going to break some eggs."[3] *James Marcus, Amazon employee number 55*

- "(Elon Musk) is impatient and demanding and doesn't accept that problems can't be solved. He's also admirably nerdy... Nothing makes Musk happier than dealing with technical issues and big-picture challenges that require complex engineering solutions."[4] *Matthew DeBord, technology writer*

- "Personality tests given to key execs (have) repeatedly shown (Michael) Dell to be an off-the-charts introvert. At its heart is Dell's belief that the status quo is never good enough, even if it means painful changes for the man with his name on the door. When success is achieved, it's greeted with five seconds of praise followed by five hours of postmortem on what could have been done better."[5] *Andrew Park, technology writer*

- "[Reid] is not particularly well organized. But perhaps his day-to-day chaos partially enables his creativity. Creativity involves connecting disparate ideas. The man is a non-stop generator of ideas—perhaps the unstructured tempo of his life is a positive enabling force."[6] *Ben Casnocha, coauthor with Reid Hoffman of* The Start-up of You: Adapt to the Future, Invest in Yourself and Transform Your Career

- "Reid is not a business-running kind of guy. He likes to take off his shoes, think of the world broadly and not worry about corporate

---

[3] Streitfeld, David, and Christine Haughney. "Expecting the Unexpected From Jeff Bezos." *The New York Times*, The New York Times, 17 Aug. 2013, www.nytimes.com/2013/08/18/business/expecting-the-unexpected-from-jeff-bezos.html.

[4] DeBord, Matthew. "Why Elon Musk Isn't 'Deeply Flawed' in His Personality." *Business Insider.* 11 December 2015, www.businessinsider.com/why-elon-musk-isnt-deeply-flawed-in-his-personality-2015-12.

[5] Park, Andrew. "What You Don't Know About Dell." Bloomberg.com. November 03, 2003. https://www.bloomberg.com/news/articles/2003-11-02/what-you-dont-know-about-dell.

[6] Casnocha, Ben. "10,000 Hours with Reid Hoffman: What I Learned." http://casnocha.com/reid-hoffman-lessons.

spend and margins."[7] *David Siminoff, Silicon Valley investor and entrepreneur*

- "Reed Hastings has a restless, slightly paranoid attitude, combined with a Steve Jobs-like perfectionist streak"[8] *John Doerr, partner at Kleiner Perkins Caufield Byers*

Clearly, there is no standard set of behaviors disruptive leaders are expected to adhere to, and these few examples make clear how contradictory and complex these individuals can be: visionary, murderous, goofy, nerdy, technical, complex, solution-oriented, introverted, critical, intellectual, nonlinear, chaotic, restless, unbusinesslike, laid-back, paranoid, perfectionist, and on and on.

Given the chaos that a big and audacious disruption can leash, it is quite natural that those of us who feel we have a lot to lose from a disruptive event will fight hard against it, questioning the disruptive leader's ethics or whether his or her ego is getting ahead of the game. Unfortunately, any large-scale disruption is going to produce winners and losers, and disruptive leaders are almost always lightning rods for controversy.

Most disruptive leaders have no problem thinking outside the box, and many actively push the boundaries of what society considers to be ethically and legally correct at the time. But the course of history has shown that yesterday's moral frameworks are swept aside by the next generation's view of what is right and ethical.

Large egos are not always welcome by society, and disruptive leaders need to have a healthy ego in the face of resistance. But truly great leaders understand the importance of keeping their egos from getting in the way of being open-minded and learning during the process of a big, audacious disruption. These leaders replace ego with confidence.

---

[7] Rusli, Evelyn M. "A King of Connections Is Tech's Go-To Guy." *The New York Times.* November 05, 2011. http://www.nytimes.com/2011/11/06/business/reid-hoffman-of-linkedin-has-become-the-go-to-guy-of-tech.html.

[8] Copeland, Michael V. "Reed Hastings: Leader of the Pack." *Fortune.* November 18, 2010. http://fortune.com/2010/11/18/reed-hastings-leader-of-the-pack/.

Of course, there are plenty of traditional business leaders and executives with little interest in being "disruptive" who have at one time or another behaved like the men highlighted above. For that reason I have put together a list of nine characteristics that make the most successful disruptive leaders distinctive and different. Some I've already discussed, and others will become clearer later.

1. **They are "brainiacs."** Some famous disruptors never finish college, while others receive PhDs from the highest-ranked universities in the world. But they all have the same commitment to lifelong learning. Disruptive CEOs can easily transition from logical reasoning to more creative, visual, and nonlinear ways of thinking while synthesizing disparate parts into something original and new.

2. **They often push accepted behavioral, cultural, legal, and ethical boundaries to the limit.** Unfortunately, if some of their more extreme tendencies aren't reined in properly, they can quickly destroy everything they and their team worked hard to build.

3. **They've learned how to disrupt their own frames of reference and unproductive mindsets.** This helps them increase their focus, ability to innovate, and to stay one step ahead of would-be competitors. Disruptive leaders expect and often demand their teams to think and act in the same way.

4. **They look for information, insights, and inspiration in unexpected places.** They recognize that data is by nature backward-looking and hence of limited value in a world that is being (re-) created. Great disruptors ask excellent questions *and* listen carefully to the answers because they never know when someone else might have an insight that could be useful to them and the business.

5. **Their businesses—regardless of whether they are B2C or B2B—deliver on at least one of three fundamental value propositions:**

   - Provide goods, services and experiences that were previously only available to the most privileged members of society to a much larger percentage of the population more easily and affordably.

   - Give customers what they want, when they want it and how they want it.

   - Eliminate or reduce the things in people's everyday lives they don't want, from everyday annoyances like wasted time, boredom, complexity or unhappiness as well as life-threatening situations like poverty and disease.

6. **They understand that successful business disruptions have to be planned and executed very strategically: more stays the same than changes.** The Tesla car—at least to date—has changed almost nothing about the average car's interior or exterior or the way we drive, except it has made high-end cars less reliant on fossil fuel. Uber and Lyft have completely disrupted taxi and limousine companies around the world by simply making it possible to order car service via cell phones.

7. **Their businesses have short-term negative consequences for many other companies, competitors, and businesspeople.** Some existing organizations are driven out of business, and many individual careers are adversely affected. However, the value created for billions of people far outweighs such negative incidents.

8. **They build companies that successfully implement their ideas.** Disruptive enterprises have the funding necessary to execute their plans. They have the right people doing the right jobs with the wherewithal and commitment to push through

many breakdowns and hurdles. Their organizations are agile and able to shift quickly, even as they grow by implementing key processes and structures.

9. **They generate unimaginable wealth for themselves, their investors, their employees, and others connected to their companies.** The stock market rewarded Amazon with an almost 5,000 percent increase within two years of the company's 1997 initial public offering (IPO). As Lou Gerstner successfully disrupted and turned around IBM, the company's market capitalization rose from $29 billion in 1993, when he was hired, to $168 billion in 2002, when he retired. On the other hand, during the period when Howard Stringer led Sony and wasn't willing or able to disrupt anything at the company of any significance, Sony's stock lost 75 percent of its value.

SECTION 6

Smaller Disruptors

U p to this point, I've focused on well-known disruptive leaders who either have built or run large multi-national companies, mostly in the technology sector. But there are thousands of less well-known entrepreneurs and business people planning and building disruptive companies in just about every industry segment imaginable. Many of these companies will stay small intentionally or unintentionally.

For example, the real estate industry isn't exactly the first sector one thinks of in the context of big, audacious disruptions. But in New York City the business of real estate comes closest to what the earth must have been like in its primordial stage—turbulent volcanoes spewing molten lava, monster beings wreaking havoc wherever they roam, and few signs of higher intelligence. New York real estate is never at ease, and even the most powerful at some point get disrupted and either disrupt themselves or die.

The real estate brokerage business is highly fragmented and most firms are relatively small. One of the best-known real estate brokerage firms currently being disrupted by an upstart company is the Corcoran Group, the real estate behemoth built by *Shark Tank* star Barbara Corcoran, now headed by Pamela Liebman.[9] It is under attack by Compass, a well-funded real estate tech start-up that has been raiding Corcoran's offices. Hundreds of senior managing directors and high-profile agents have left Corcoran to join Compass.

Corcoran also claims some of the defecting agents have hijacked its proprietary systems, including its listings databases. This follows hot on

---

[9] Clarke, Katherine. "Huge NYC Brokerage under Attack from a Start-up: Suit." *NY Daily News.* March 23, 2015. http://www.nydailynews.com/life-style/real-estate/nyc-largest-brokerage-attack-start-up-suit-article-1.2159866.

the heels of Compass having stolen trade secrets from and hacked the database of rental giant Citi Habitats.

Compass, founded by tech entrepreneur Ori Allon and Goldman Sachs alum Robert Reffkin, was still in start-up mode in 2016, but it already touted a valuation of $360 million, having attracted investment from business titans such as American Express CEO Kenneth Chenault and Joshua Kushner (Jared Kushner's brother) of Thrive Capital.

To say the American health care industry is in a period of massive disruption, meanwhile, would be an understatement. But what is particularly interesting is that a lot of the disruption is coming from smaller start-ups, including many run by minorities and women.

Sheila Lirio Marcelo was born and raised in the Philippines, growing up in an entrepreneurial household. She graduated magna cum laude from Mt. Holyoke College with a degree in economics and earned MBA and JD degrees with honors, along with the Dean's Award from Harvard University.

Marcelo first stumbled upon the challenges many mothers face after she had her first child, Ryan. As an immigrant and a student, she didn't have a support system in the form of family nearby; later, her father suffered a heart attack while helping care for her second child, and she had difficulties finding help to care for him as well as her two young sons. Marcelo realized there was a need in the market to help families find care resources, but waited five years to launch a start-up, gaining operational and managerial experience in the intervening years.

Care.com, founded in 2006, addresses the unique care needs of each family through every stage of their lives—helping families select childcare, senior care, special needs care, tutoring, pet care, housekeeping, and more. The site includes prescreened profiles, monitored messaging, access to background checks, recorded references, and educational information on the interviewing process.

From 2006 through August 2012, Care.com raised more than $110 million in venture capital from investors including LinkedIn's Reid Hoffman. Marcelo is one of the few female technology entrepreneurs to raise more than $35 million in venture capital funding. The company went public January 24, 2014, and today has more than 26.4 million members in twenty countries.

I've had the good fortune of meeting and working with several men and women who have at one point or another have had to disrupt themselves, their business, a competitor or even an industry. While their companies are small and not as well-known as those mentioned above, they have been very successful in their own right:

- Al weathered two major financial corrections (1987 and 2001) and the crisis of 2008 in addition to several life-altering events as he built what is today a well-respected and highly profitable wealth management business.

- After a very successful career in banking, Rob left the world of large financial institutions. His new business is committed to disrupting and correcting the inherent problems in the current system of fixed-income trading. He has a great team, key strategic partnerships, and the funding necessary to achieve his goals.

- My friend Dov has been a successful entrepreneur for decades and has now built a company committed to transforming the way post-hospital therapy is delivered.

Their stories, along with those of members of my Vistage group and my private clients—as well as a few business folks who didn't become clients of mine—appear throughout the rest of the book to highlight various key points. I hope you are as inspired by them as I am and learn a few things along the way.[10]

Take the free online assessment at **www.JohnFFurth.com/diagnostics** to find out how disruptive you are as a leader. But remember— anyone can actively develop themselves—this is just a snapshot of your current capabilities.

---

[10] Vistage is a membership-based organization and I am one of over 1000 Chairs in the world. A Chair's job is to form groups of between twelve and twenty local CEOs and business owners who are looking for a peer-to-peer experience to solve problems and uncover opportunities.

PART TWO

DISRUPT YOURSELF BEFORE YOU DISRUPT OTHERS

SECTION 7

It Starts with You

At the core of everyone's personal and professional journey lies a set of beliefs that start forming the minute we are born. Events occur along the way that cause us to question assumptions about ourselves and the world, often forcing us to replace those assumptions with new ones that will help us better achieve our goals. Teachers, leaders, coaches or consultants inspire us to seek higher truths. (In fact, we first experience what it means to disrupt ourselves when we start the process of education, given that the act of learning is all about continuously replacing mindsets with ideas that might prove to be more useful for the future.) In the wake of negative experiences we wonder if "the system" is really working in our favor or whether it needs to be disrupted. The best of us rise to the challenge and change situations that are unsustainable.

Maybe because of my education, my parents, or my own ambitions, I understood early on that personal and professional fulfillment was predicated on how much I was willing to reevaluate myself, my beliefs, and my view of the world at regular intervals. If I hadn't put myself through three or four major life-changing events and a series of smaller disruptions, my life would have been far less rich and wonderful. I'm only fifty-eight and hope this continual process of learning and growing will never end.

The first active disruption was entirely my decision. I went back to school to get an MBA at the age of twenty-eight after being a musician in Germany. Despite leaving the country I had called home for eight years, ending a relationship that I had been in for most of that time, and having to learn a whole new set of skills, it was, relatively speaking, an easy undertaking. I had a clear vision of why I was doing this and what I wanted to become.

After a one-and-a-half-year stint at Deutsche Bank, I disrupted *that* path and became a consultant when the bank bought the leading European strategy consulting firm at the time, Roland Berger. After years of professional uncertainty, I had found the perfect fit. I was working at the highest levels of business solving strategic and operational issues important to CEOs and their C-suite executives. My teams and I were there to help leaders make the right decisions in the face of uncertainty and complexity. I was on a roll, and it felt like heaven.

I capped my two-decade career with a stint as the CEO and President of the trade association for the consulting industry, the Association of Management Consulting Firms (AMCF). But the industry was changing—high-end strategy consulting wasn't growing as a segment, and large, one-stop-shop monoliths like IBM, Accenture, and the Big Four accounting firms were taking over. I had also grown and matured as an individual. The psychological and emotional payoff was wearing thin, and I felt I was stagnating as a professional and leader.

I decided a few years ago there had to be a better way to make a positive impact on leaders and their companies and proceeded to disrupt and transform myself yet again.

This time it was anything but easy. Even though I believed I had thought through this decision in great detail, I didn't realize the extent to which I was going to have to confront a lot of behaviors and attitudes that had not only slowed me down over the preceding years but also were negatively influencing my personal relationships. Particularly painful was dealing with my almost obsessive need to be right under all circumstances—an occupational hazard for most consultants—and to deflect responsibility for a lot of my actions. It took me years to fully comprehend and change these ways of being.

I stopped accepting assignments that required me to do certain tasks that had at one time defined me as a "high-end" consultant but which could now be done more easily and cheaply by younger consultants or off-shore resources. This included intensive research-based work and producing reams of documents and presentations. I knew, however, that I wanted to continue doing the parts I enjoyed most—formulating and maintaining close and trusted client relationships, developing solutions that were creative and strategic and working on a wide variety of topics. I also came to realize that I had twenty-five years of valuable experience as a leader and CEO which I could draw on to help business leaders.

That process led me to become more of a business coach than a consultant. Coaches are supposed to get into the trenches with their clients and actively help them achieve results. Good coaches don't need to deliver reams of paper to validate their recommendations because they are trained to draw the answers out of their clients and not simply tell them what to do. Coaches can go places psychologically and emotionally where consultants are not always allowed (or even well-equipped) to go.

And indeed, this reinvention has made my work much more meaningful and relevant. I no longer feel bogged down by the need to be the smartest guy in the room. I have also learned to challenge clients far more effectively than before. This has made it much easier to get them to change their frames of reference, so they recognize—and eventually implement—opportunities they may never have considered or believed possible.

I want my clients to have the same liberating, productive, and transformative experiences I've had and will hopefully continue to have during my life and career. Even more importantly, I want them to understand they are the only ones responsible for making their lives and businesses as successful and fulfilling as possible so they and no one else own their tomorrows.

SECTION 8

Unproductive Mindsets and Behaviors

One of the aspects that I love most about what I do is getting to meet a diverse group of entrepreneurs and leaders of small to medium-sized businesses (SMBs) on a regular basis. Many of them are based near where I live and have that unique New York City mix of earthiness, wiliness, and sophistication. While there are a lot of stubborn and frustrating—and a few truly crazy—people in this city, there are also many born storytellers eagerly waiting for an audience like me.

In early 2016, I met the owners of two prominent companies in New York City's taxi and limousine industry who fit that description to a tee. One was a woman who owns and runs one of the city's premier limousine services which is based in south Brooklyn. The other is one of New York City's largest taxi medallion holders and brokers.

They had no trouble telling me how Uber, Lyft, and other disruptive companies—seemingly without so much as a shrug from NYC regulators—were devastating their businesses. And yet, for all their accomplishments and business savvy, I was surprised that both these entrepreneurs had allowed themselves to be stopped dead in their tracks. Revenues had plunged and formerly healthy margins had all but disappeared, threatening everything they had worked hard to build over their entire adult lives.

It was also clear to me very early in our conversations that they weren't about to take advice from someone outside their industry, preferring instead to stick to what they knew. They are interesting examples of what can happen when perilous and unproductive mindsets like the few listed below take over.

I'm Always the Smartest in the Room

The Brooklyn-based businesswoman explained to me how she had always been at the top of her class in school and college. Like a modern-day Cassandra, she was constantly warning her colleagues and competitors about the dangers of Uber and Lyft with little effect. "I knew what was happening, but it was like talking to a brick wall," she said.

But instead of taking the opportunity to make changes to her business, she had done nothing beyond forecasting death, doom and destruction. Six years later, she was in danger of literally driving both herself and her company over the cliff.

Although not quite as prescient as our Cassandra of the taxi and limousine industry, the gentleman who owns the largest taxi medallion brokerage in New York City is in fact originally from Greece. He had started his professional life in the city twenty-five years earlier as a taxi driver before he started building his business. He is charismatic and can talk a very good game; he also spent a lot of time telling me how smart *he* was.

But the kicker came when he said he was making $78 million in revenue annually but had racked up $100 million in debt buying and selling the medallions taxi drivers need to own and drive New York City taxis. In the previous five years, the value of these medallions had dropped to about one-fifth of the price they had commanded in the years before Uber, Lyft, and others entered the scene.

He had also taken no preemptive action to rethink his business model and allowed the situation to go on endlessly, thinking at some point he would be able to fix the problem—until it was too late.

He then explained with a flourish that he was working with Goldman Sachs—the smartest of the smartest—to solve the problem by restructuring his company.

These two business owners might have been smarter than me, but at least I had a business that was thriving and growing.

I'll Wait until the Storm Blows over

Owners of businesses subject to back-and-forth swings in politics and regulations find it hard to commit to significant change when they can't figure out what's brewing in the halls of power. They often make do with a wait-and-see strategy. While this can sometimes be a reasonable and productive choice, it also can be simply an excuse for inaction.

Both entrepreneurs above were part of various organizations tied to the NYC Taxi and Limousine Commission and were involved in efforts to convince regulators to make decisions that would help them. They hesitated to make too many drastic changes to their businesses, such as investing in mobile technology with similar functionality to that of Uber or hedging their exposure using more sophisticated financial instruments. They just hoped things would go back to the way they used to be once the regulators woke up and righted their wrongs.

Unfortunately, that never happened.

I'm Just Too Nice

After an hour of frustrating conversation, the owner of the limousine service in South Brooklyn walked over to a cat sunning itself in the window of her office. She petted it, looked through a hole that had once been the window that allowed her to watch the garage where her people worked, and wistfully said: "You know, I'm just too nice." This, after she had yelled at her people to shut up so she and I could hear each other talk.

Maybe she *was* too nice. The situation clearly was so bad for her that she was losing sight in one eye, had been in the hospital for several ailments, and was struggling with a son who was addicted to drugs. Perhaps if she hadn't been "so nice," she might've been able to enjoy her life more than she was.

Maybe I'm Not Really That Good at This

Sometimes, unresolved personal issues can hamper otherwise talented individuals' abilities to achieve the goals they set for themselves.

Alex is the son of Ecuadorian immigrants. For a highly intelligent, motivated boy who was highly attuned to his surroundings, it was not an easy life growing up, and Alex was determined to create a better and more meaningful existence. He quickly became an overachiever, excelling at whatever he put his mind to. Alex eventually applied to the top fourteen colleges in the United States and was accepted by every one of them, finally choosing to go to Harvard.

Alex's first job after school was as an analyst with a real estate fund in Houston. He left this position after just two years because making a lot of money without giving back to society—especially to help younger people who were dealing with some of the same difficulties he had been through—was untenable for Alex.

He landed a job in New York City heading up operations for a charter school. Two years later, at the age of twenty-six, Alex started his own construction real estate company with the mission of building the best schools possible, especially those serving underprivileged children. I met Alex just as he turned 30.

During our initial discussions, it was clear that Alex was not as free of those early childhood experiences as he had hoped to be. He was still struggling with deeply held but unproductive beliefs about himself, his background, and what that meant for his future. He often let his emotional state get in the way to such a degree that it incapacitated him for days.

Every little thing that went wrong was a major blow to his ego and he'd go down in a spiral of insecurity and depression, further convincing himself of his unworthiness. By the time we met, Alex was doubtful his business would ever be able to generate more than $1 or $2 million in revenue. He also painted a picture of himself as a loner and a weird guy who would never marry or have children.

When talking to such an articulate and bright young man, any halfway-intelligent person could see this mindset was preposterous. Alex was a star—highly intelligent, compassionate and driven—but he was doing everything possible at that point to limit himself and his power.

Alex quickly signed up to become the first member of my burgeoning Vistage group, but our first coaching session didn't go as planned for either of us. I listened carefully to Alex, and all I could think was how great this young man's future could be if he just got over himself. Suddenly I couldn't hold myself back. I read him the riot act.

If he wanted to fritter away his hard work, intelligence, and goals and be miserable his entire life, I told him, then he should go ahead, but not on my watch. There was absolutely no reason in the world why he couldn't make tens, even hundreds of millions of dollars, have meaningful relationships, and be happy.

Alex was speechless and meekly said he didn't think that was what our session was going to be like. A sudden grip of fear seized me. Had I gone too far?

I decided he needed some time to think and took the opportunity to get him a book from my office that would clarify in better words what I might have expressed so crudely. Alex was very quiet when I came back. I gave him the book and he left. I was sure I was going to get a call that he didn't want to continue working with me.

About a week later I got the dreaded call. But instead of quitting, Alex thanked me profusely for making it clear to him how he was sabotaging his business and his life. Within twelve months of that first session, Alex has gone on to double his company's revenue, hire several full-time staff, extend his network within both the real estate and Latino worlds in New York City, and meet and marry a girl he is crazy about. He now has money in the bank and is actively pursuing investors to back his real passion, which is to build affordable housing that is green, attractive to look at, and improves the lives of the residents who live there.

After that first conversation, our coaching sessions became more measured and thoughtful, but also less risky for him and for me. One day, Alex unexpectedly asked me when we were going to have another great session like the first one. He wanted me to be *more* challenging.

That was an important break-through moment for me—never hold back with the greatly talented. If they aren't continuously pushed to grow, they move on quickly. I'm happy to say that two years later, Alex is growing stronger and more confident in his future every day.

SECTION 9

Confusing Disruption with Destruction

There are many businesspeople who like to think of themselves as disruptors when they're actually more in danger of being destructive than disruptive.

Millions of entrepreneurs have weathered the multiple course corrections that occur during most start-up phases and just assume that's the way it will always be. Many find it hard to accept that what their organizations might need most is stability, well-defined processes and organizational structures, as well as an inspirational mission to thrive and grow. Paradoxically, these business leaders also need to learn the power of disruption—but a disruption to their overly disruptive behaviors. Unfortunately, many don't understand this until it's too late and they've destroyed their companies.

My client, Sean, is a perfect example of a businessman who was headed in that direction before we started working together. About ten years before we met, he had founded a consulting firm to help risk managers and their teams develop and deliver successful international risk programs. Sean is highly creative and intelligent, and at some point, he convinced himself that if his company could be more innovative than his competitors, he would be better positioned to build a sustainable base of clients and revenue.

That sounds good in theory, but there's one big problem with that assumption. Sean's target client base of risk managers at large multinational companies are for the most part conservative and not particularly open to new ideas that have not been properly tested and assessed. In fact, their job title says it all—risk managers are paid to *lessen risks* to their organizations, not increase them with unproven approaches. But for ten years, Sean had defended his point of view against all the odds.

Sean was an army officer, and then a risk management consultant at Ernst & Young before establishing his own firm. Once he got his company off the ground, he quickly got tired of the wear-and-tear of consulting. Sean was hungry for faster growth. He had also discovered that his target clients were increasingly shifting spending away from consulting to software as a better and cheaper way to manage complex projects across many countries.

Sean quite logically decided that he needed to follow the money, so he changed the focus of the company in its third year of operations to basic software and hired a few technologists and software engineers. He also let natural attrition run its course as his consultants left for more promising opportunities elsewhere. Unfortunately, a few went to his main competitors and even took some of his clients with them.

Then the great recession hit in 2008, and with little to show for the investments he had made in software, Sean jettisoned that approach and went back to just offering risk management consulting services. With most of his former consulting team gone, he depended on an army of contractors to do the work, even though they were so expensive that the company netted no profit after paying them.

Slowly but surely, Sean brought the necessary expertise back in-house and tried to replicate the success they had with his largest client with other clients. When that also didn't happen the way he had hoped, Sean decided he should build a company that offered both software and consulting services. If nothing else, Sean reasoned, he would at least have more ammunition to fire at potential clients.

But by that time, however, the damage had been done. The sudden shifts over the previous years had not only destabilized his organization but had also confused his clients. At some point, many of them probably started losing trust in him and his company. Other than the firm's biggest client, which most years represented as much as 85 percent of the company's revenue, new clients were signing on for smaller and smaller projects. Slowly, Sean lost confidence and retreated within himself. The company began to look and feel more like a think tank and not the disruptive, innovative, and energetic company he had originally wanted to build.

About two years before we started working together, Sean hired a new manager, Jeremy, to run the technology and creative services side of his business. Jeremy was immediately successful and built his group quickly, but he also realized that the organization was not sustainable in its current form and Sean, as the founder and CEO, needed outside help and objectivity. He convinced Sean to join my Vistage group and Sean, in turn, promoted Jeremy to be his second-in-command.

Sean appears at first to be someone in control and clear about his intentions and strategy for the company. He is polite, articulate, well-read, and recognized as a thought leader in his chosen field of expertise, operational risk management. Unfortunately, his ability to face down danger and not let it show—after all, he was an officer in the Army—made it very difficult to get through to him in the beginning. Sean just felt a dull ache and struggled to let his guard down. He also couldn't really understand why his "logical disruptions" hadn't worked.

The first sign that Sean's mindset wasn't in the right place was his insistence that the only thing a CEO should care about is sales and revenue. I countered by saying the number one priority for any successful CEO should be his organization. Now, it's true that even the most senior partners in consulting companies are on the hook for generating revenue, but they're not salespeople. They're experts with large networks of clients who they have made successful. Even then, the CEOs of most consulting firms don't actively generate revenue; they hire and manage employees and partners who do that.

But the turning point that convinced Sean he needed to disrupt a lot of his beliefs about himself was a video he produced to market his company.

At the time, a lot of entrepreneurs were using funny and provocative videos to cut through the noise on social media and grab the attention of a huge consumer base. Seizing on what he thought was a great opportunity,

Sean went ahead and produced and distributed such a video. It was very polished and well-made, but it bombed with his generally cautious and not particularly creative client base. It just didn't resonate with them, and I'm sure in some cases they might have even been offended.

Shortly thereafter, Sean's largest client announced they were going to spend less money on services from his company in the years to come. When that happened, Sean couldn't ignore what Jeremy and I, or anyone else, were saying any longer.

Sean now understands how important it is to ask questions and listen carefully to his clients and the marketplace. He has calmed down considerably and is more open to accepting that many of his whims and short-term ideas are less than productive and could put the firm back in danger. He's learned the power of disrupting his old way of thinking and doing things and now uses many of the methodologies he has seen work at Vistage with his own clients.

SECTION 10

Fear and Fearlessness

For hundreds of thousands of years, human beings experienced fear as a direct result of physical threats in the external world which compelled us to take immediate action. Tiger approaching, run fast! Food, eat it! Angry man approaching with knife, fight!

Thus, people who feared the right things survived to pass on their genes. In so doing, the trait of fear and the response to it were selected as beneficial to the race.

Even though wild animals, scarcity of food, and hand-to-hand combat have all but disappeared for many people, we are still confronted every day with potentially life-threatening risks. Fear plays a dominant and positive force in our lives by reminding us to look both ways before crossing the street, avoid dangerous areas at night, drive carefully, and so on.

These are the good fears that push us into action when the very existence of our businesses, families, or communities is seriously threatened.

Unfortunately, modern life with all its complexity and ambiguity has also produced a set of fears which are often irrational and unproductive, such as the fear of looking stupid, the fear of rejection, the fear of change, and on and on. And for some CEOs, the fear of being unveiled as an imposter or fraud can be so overwhelming that they sabotage themselves every chance they get.

These fears have the power to alter our perception of reality to such an extent that even the brightest and toughest among us can find it difficult to make the right choices and decisions. Our survival instinct gets neutralized and we become blind to the potential dangers to our personal and professional existence. That's when we run the risk of being tripped up by events we're no longer capable of recognizing until it's too late.

Because professional people tend to be well-educated and logical beings, our rational brains often kick in when something unexpectedly bad happens, or even worse, we form and reinforce beliefs about the world that often get expressed in highly negative terms. We convince ourselves that we can never let something like that ever happen again. We stop actively looking for business opportunities and start making decisions that come back to haunt us later. Some of us simply give up when faced with these fears.

Over the years I have developed a question-based methodology to help me unearth the fears, points of view, or mindsets that get in the way of my clients' happiness and success in both their businesses and personal lives. When potential clients hear about my methodology, they often jokingly remark that it sounds a lot like psychotherapy. And indeed, there are many elements of this approach in a one-to-one setting that are very similar.

But I am neither a psychiatrist nor a psychologist; I am a business coach. I focus on behaviors and mindsets that get in the way of desired outcomes. Should I detect deeper and more damaging psychological or physical problems, I will refer a client to an appropriate doctor.

I listen carefully for stories that contradict other things that client has said, are downright unbelievable, or just plain wrong from a business point of view. Sometimes it's a passing comment about someone or an event that a client has clearly not processed properly. Especially telling are behaviors and actions that are repeated over and over again, yet never produce the desired results. When something catches my attention, I immediately drill down until we get to something deeper and truer.

Often, clients will push back or get defensive because of the pain. This is a natural reaction and doesn't mean they are not open to disruption, change, or transformation. It just means I have to work a little harder to get at what's really going on inside them.

Those who are fundamentally open to improving themselves and their businesses will take the opportunity to talk through the issues. The weight starts to fall off their shoulders as they understand how a particular issue has been causing problems for them. Once that occurs, I know I have successfully disrupted their mindsets. Doors suddenly open, a light gets turned on, and their creative juices and energy return quickly. Decisions become easier and clients feel more confident in their ability to plan and produce a future in line with their expectations.

Once clients have experienced what it's like to disrupt themselves, we then begin the process of determining what exactly *they* are going to do to disrupt their businesses and the industries of which they are a part. I help them understand that true, meaningful disruption may be painful to them or somebody else in the short-term, but in the long run it is one of the surest ways to renew their power, energy, and creativity and can help them transform their companies more effectively and create more value for their customers and their companies.

It's almost impossible to recognize a problem and solve it without the help of an external party. Until you find someone you can work with, many of the misguided mindsets you've put in place will get in the way of your performance and/or produce results that are below what you expect or want. This external perspective doesn't necessarily have to come from a coach; it can also originate with a second-in-command, a spouse, or a group of peers, as long as they don't come with an agenda of their own.

I would suggest using the methodology outlined above as a sort of checklist to determine whether somebody has the necessary outside perspective and expertise to help you. You also should be comfortable enough with a person to share some of your most personal concerns and experiences.

Be open, vulnerable, and willing to be challenged. If the work is going well, in about three or four months you should notice that things will start shifting for you in a meaningful way.

If for some reason you can't or don't want to find someone to work with, then think back on moments in your personal or professional life when you felt compelled to make a sudden shift. Maybe you switched schools, changed careers, changed the focus of your business, or ended a relationship. Try to recall what led up to making that decision and understand how the context changed around you and what it felt like when the light finally went off in your head.

Go back to those moments of illumination when you finally grasped a new concept or process, either because you read something or were taking a class of great importance to you. Maybe it was the result of a random conversation. Something went *click,* and suddenly a lot of things made sense and you were back in the saddle, ready to continue the journey.

The leaders who understand the power of disruption actively use these painful events to cause the kind of breakthroughs that help them become better leaders and human beings. They know that this productive and life-enhancing form of fearlessness is the foundation upon which they can build organizations that can have maximum impact on the world and our standard of living.

Stuck in the same place personally or professionally unable to find a way forward? Contact us at **www.JohnFFurth.com** and we'll help you get moving again.

PART THREE

MAKING GREAT
DECISIONS IN A
DISRUPTIVE WORLD

SECTION 11

From the Simple to the Very Complex

Internal data often provides the first warning signs that something isn't quite right at a company. But even then, human nature is such that these warning signals might still not be enough for a call to action—or worse, they can also be a call for the wrong action. Additional information—especially external data—is often needed to truly understand the nature and magnitude of a problem, make the right kind of decisions and build a plan to tackle those issues.

A company's board will sometimes push for the right response. In theory, board directors have access to many external insights a CEO often may not have or is blind to. The board should, in theory, have a broader view of the situation. But in recent years, a rise in stakeholder and proxy-analyst pressures has made directors sensitive to any decision that might provoke a negative reaction from the media, proxy-advisory firms, institutional analysts, and/or activist investors. In addition, directors too often put self-preservation ahead of shareholder interests. They like their board seats—it gives them some prestige. In short, many boards are just too risk-adverse to stomach a major disruption that could put them at risk.

The need for change can bubble up from within an organization, especially when business unit heads, internal strategy teams, and/or marketing folks clearly demonstrate a need for disruption.

Unfortunately, many employees have the same attitude as some boards of directors—they want to keep their jobs. Leaders of small and medium-size businesses often find it just as difficult to make decisions as their counterparts at larger institutions and to gain the necessary insights into their businesses, their competitors, and customers. But the difficulties are significantly different and go beyond the comparative sizes of the businesses.

With luck, some SMBs can survive for years without access to significant amounts of internal or external data, relying instead on the charisma of their leaders, weak competition, or extensive and supportive networks, for example. Thus, employees at most SMBs are not trained in or even aware of the basics of management reporting, analysis, and transformational thinking.

In addition, many of the resources and highly developed ecosystems available to large corporations, which help leaders and their employees learn valuable skills, find the right experts, and pay for external data and literature, are not available to small business. And unlike the more business like cultures at bigger companies, the family-like environments that small company leaders and entrepreneurs tend to develop and foster can sometimes pose a unique challenge to making significant change.

Many clients come to me with only a vague sense of what's going on in their companies. They often know there's a big problem: usually, they can't grow their business, they're losing money, or they're having problems with their employees. But they find it difficult to understand the root cause of the problem and wonder why nothing seems to work.

Others state emphatically that they know exactly what they need to do, and yet they just don't do it.

When data is scarce, expensive to obtain, or not available in digital form, the only alternative left is to rely on oneself or others who have experience gained through the years. In such cases, leaders rely on intuition, which is the label given to this style of inference and decision making.

Unfortunately, as often as intuition can be right, it can also lead to wrong decisions.

I often use simple illustrations like the one below to help my clients understand the difference between decisions that can be made using basic business instinct and more decisions that require sophisticated judgment capabilities and multiple perspectives. The more complex and important the decision is, the more a CEO needs to think through a variety of factors, inputs and points of view to come to the right conclusions.

Handling Increasingly Important and Complex Decisions

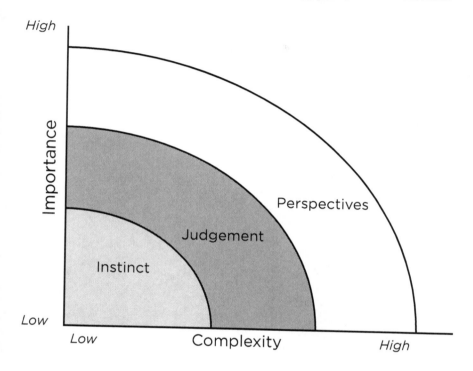

However, in disruptive environments where new ground is forged every day, and time and money can run out quickly, there are two additional factors that complicate decision-making: urgency and the high level of uncertainty about the outcomes of many important decisions.

CEOs who don't have to rush to make particularly important or complex decisions and who have a high degree of certainty about the outcomes of those decisions are probably not living in disruptive worlds. In fact, they run a high risk of becoming complacent and being disrupted themselves.

Nonchallenging Decision-making Environments

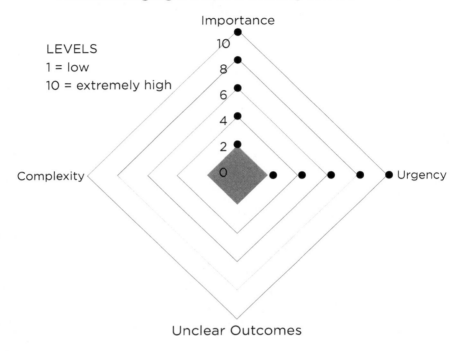

It's often very hard for a business leader to tell if his or her prior experience or fine-tuned executive judgment are of any help in highly disruptive environments. In high stress situations, where every decision seems important, complex, urgent, or uncertain, reverting to past paradigms can even be potentially harmful.

High Stress Decision-making Environments

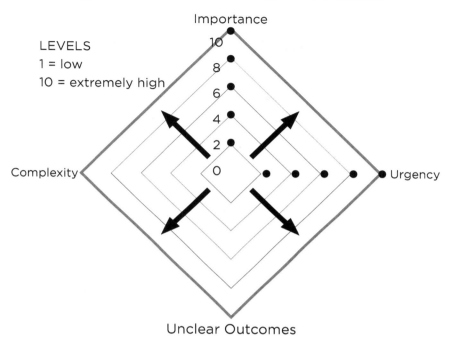

High Stress Decision-making Environments

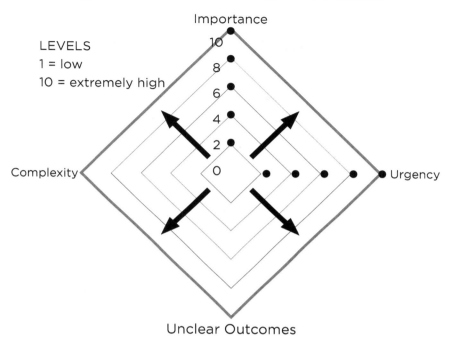

In the following sections, I'll provide you with some disruptive and original ideas to help you find important data and perspectives about your business and the external world from a variety of traditional and nontraditional sources.

While this information may not actually decrease the importance or urgency of a particular decision, having access to multiple data points and perspectives will provide the foundation for great decisions. I will also suggest a number of tools and techniques to help you and/or your team break down the complexity of a decision into manageable pieces. It's my hope these ideas will reduce the anxiety of tackling big, audacious decisions—or at least make you more comfortable with the doubt and uncertainty of decisions, especially in disruptive environments.

Using Judgement and Multiple Perspectives

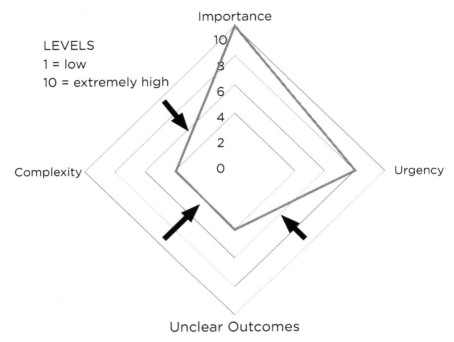

SECTION 12

External Perspectives

Most leaders tend to go back to the same places when looking for input and ideas for important decisions, because those founts of wisdom have worked well before. Large companies have formidable research and development facilities to develop new technologies, skunkworks to test how these technologies can be put together for new products, teams of strategists and management consultants to dream up new business models, and marketing professionals to tell them how receptive the defined set of buyers are to a new product or service.

However, these legions of well-organized and smart employees often don't have the necessary disruptive mindset and ability to think beyond what they've been doing for years.

The alternative, which is to go out into the world in search of knowledge and inspiration, can be very disturbing if you don't have the right mindset. The fact is that despite the ubiquity of every conceivable kind of data and information and increasingly easy access to that huge body of knowledge, a single human being can't begin to comprehend more than a tiny fraction of what's out there.

I'll try to make this conundrum a little clearer. Take a look at the simple picture below. It represents all the information, learning, and knowledge in the world. In technical terms, we're talking about trillions of terabytes of data.

All Information and Knowledge in the World

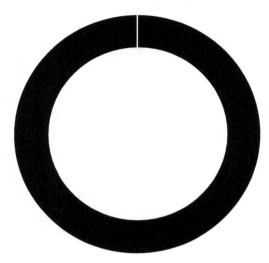

Now, look at the second version of this chart. It looks like a pie chart with two small slivers and one large piece.

All Information and Knowledge in the World

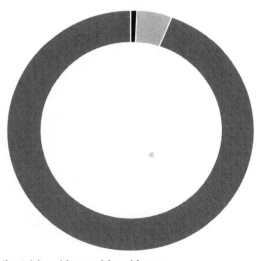

- What You Know You Know
- What You Know You Don't Know
- What You Don't Even Know You Don't Know

The first slice represents what you can *conclusively* say you know. In my case, for example, I know that I know how to speak English; I know how to drive a car, use a computer, and so on. Notice how that makes up less than 1 percent of the pie. (Even that is stretching it—it's probably more like less than 0.1 percent.)

The second slice represents the things that you can point to and say you know that you *don't* know them. For example, I know that I don't know how to fly a plane. I know that I don't know what will happen tomorrow. I can say conclusively that I don't know if there's life on other planets. This slice is a little larger—maybe around 1 to 5 percent, depending on the individual—but it's still only a fraction of everything that is known in the world.

The final slice is everything an individual *doesn't even know* he or she doesn't know. You'll notice this piece is between 95 and 99 percent of the entire pie for most people.

Precisely because you can't even conceive of what's in this third slice of knowledge and experience, you'll discover some of the greatest opportunities there. It's an amazing but scary place to be, and a truly committed disruptive leader has to be open and receptive to whatever he or she finds there, even if deeply held beliefs and ideas are overturned or even negated. Your ego needs to be left at the door.

The journey into the unknown will be chaotic and unnerving, but once you are comfortable with it—and also know at some point you have to start making decisions—you'll begin to find what you need in places you least expect. Inspiration and insights will come from industries other than your own, nature, the performing arts and entertainment, literature, and so on. A few enterprising people have built successful companies providing safe places for cutting-edge thinking and discourse, such as business schools, TED talks, the World Economic Forum, and so on.

Consultants can be useful as well—provided you pick the right one for the right reason. One consulting firm has built quite a business organizing what it calls "Innovation Safaris" to Silicon Valley or Silicon Alley. Generally, these are part of larger engagements to help client companies transform themselves using the newest technologies. Such trips occur early in a project and generate disruptive ideas among a client's leadership team in order to loosen up their creative juices and help them learn enough to be able to start putting pieces together.

Unfortunately, many of the resources mentioned above are either too expensive or not available to the average small organization. In addition, leaders of smaller businesses often find it harder than their big-company counterparts to arrange an already-packed schedule to go to many external meetings. They have to work harder to get the knowledge they need to identify and react to a disruption.

There are other resources available to SMB leaders much closer to home, and often, these are not very costly.

- Despite what Steve Jobs said to the contrary, great insights and ideas often come from a company's clients and customers. These key constituencies should always be represented in any internal strategic process, not only for the ideas and insight they generate but also because by involving them, you're already enrolling them in the possibilities being created.

  I often do customer interviews as part of strategy projects I perform as a consultant. I always remind clients that I shouldn't just interview their most loyal customers; I should also talk to those no longer actively purchasing from them. I find using in-depth customer feedback—both positive and negative—is the best way to focus a management team on what is most important. Often, simple tweaks or a few small disruptions based on the right customer feedback can lead to huge financial and market gains.

- One thing Steve Jobs *did* advocate at Apple was studying art. The company's internal training program, Apple University, teaches the same design lessons used by Picasso to create some of the most iconic and recognizable images in the history of art. One of the key concepts involves eliminating unnecessary details and boiling ideas down to only the most essential elements, as Picasso did in many of his most famous paintings.

- Biometrics or biomimicry is the practice of studying nature to find ideas. More specifically, it is the imitation of the models, systems, and elements of nature for the purpose of solving problems humans are faced with, many of which find their way into the business world.

  Living organisms have evolved well-adapted structures and materials over geological time through natural selection. Biometrics has given rise to new technologies inspired by biological solutions at the macro- and nanoscales. Humans have looked at nature for answers to problems throughout our existence. Nature has solved such engineering problems as self-healing abilities, environmental exposure tolerance and resistance, hydrophobicity, self-assembly, and harnessing solar energy.

One of the members of my Vistage group even found the inspiration to a pricing problem for which he was trying to find a disruptive solution when he went to a hamburger restaurant that offers a variety of add-on options at different price points. After ordering a hamburger laden down with condiments, proteins, and vegetables, he suddenly saw the answer he was looking for. The interesting thing is that this client owns and runs a software business. At first glance, you might wonder what Ashish could have found to inspire him at some ungodly hour in downtown Manhattan, but you never know when a light is going to come on. You just need to be open and ready for it. (The full story can be found in section 34, *Agile Experimentation.*)

It goes without saying that reading literature and books on business, leadership, and current events—really anything—is still probably one of the best ways to find ideas and inspiration. A good friend of mine with a fintech business loves to read about Michael Bloomberg's start-up pains and subsequent journey to becoming one of the great entrepreneurs of the twentieth and twenty-first centuries. This has helped my friend survive some of the greatest setbacks of his own journey and given him the inspiration to continue in even the bleakest moments.

SECTION 13

Internal Data

Only when good systems are in place can management get the kind of internal data that helps them make decisions, especially those related to day-to-day operations. Ideally this kind of data is available to senior management in the form of regular monthly financial and management reports that include carefully chosen key performance indicators (KPIs). The better a company's systems are, the more often these reports can be generated. Businesses that involve high amounts of transactions like those in the retail or stock brokerage industries sometimes need daily reports, while others get what they need from weekly or monthly reports.

Salomon is a member of my Vistage group and is an intelligent, big-hearted, intuitive business owner who loves to learn, although as a Hasidic Jew he didn't have the traditional kind of education some of my other Vistage members had. He reads a lot, especially books on leadership. These have further deepened his already high levels of integrity, willingness to give back, and ability to manage people.

For the first four years, Salomon grew his company using his instincts, experience, and a network that feeds him ideas. The problem was, he had managed his company for several years without any consistent internal data. And as you'll see in a moment, he literally paid the price for it.

The fact was that his business—a staffing company that provides physical, occupational, and speech therapists to a variety of clients and institutions—had never been profitable. Along the way, he had used up a lot of his personal savings and was close to maxing out his lines of credit and bank loans.

Salomon is very in tune with himself and those around him, and the first months working with him were a joy. He was open, vulnerable, and could play with ideas easily. However, I unfortunately realized that my initial mode of inquiry just wasn't improving the situation as I had hoped.

At the end of 2016, Salomon asked me to help him and his team with a strategic planning exercise for 2017. As soon as we started the project, it became clear to me that his biggest issue was that his current IT systems simply couldn't generate the information necessary to give him insights into the financial situation of his firm on a regular basis in an easy-to-read format without a lot of manual intervention. I asked Salomon's accountant and systems administrator to put together a pro forma P&L for 2016, so we would at least have something to get started with.

When he received that P&L, Salomon was delighted to finally have a tool he understood and could work with, but he was also shocked to see the company had generated a loss of about $0.5 million on $4.5 million of revenue. He knew the company hadn't been profitable, but it was much worse than he expected.

We developed a reporting format for monthly cash flow, P&L, and balance sheet that Salomon would receive the second or third week of the following month so he could keep tighter reins on the financial condition of the company. His systems expert worked doubly hard to get the systems to give us what we needed, but it was worth it.

With the ability to generate good financial reports much more easily, Salomon and his leadership team quickly got to the heart of what was needed to grow the organization and become profitable. They could perform more sophisticated financial analyses and readily locate unnecessary costs they could reduce through simple adjustments to the business.

Salomon set specific targets for the number and type of therapists the company needed to fulfill all of its obligations in 2017. In addition, he and his team discovered that if they increased the utilization of their therapists by an average of three or four percent—which was in the realm of possibility—they would be able to improve profitability by almost $200,000.

The energy that this data and knowledge unleashed was so tremendous that within weeks, Solomon had found and signed significant new contracts. He also hired an additional recruiter to improve the supply of therapists. Most importantly, however, Solomon now has more precise and reliable financial information to make decisions and feel more confident. He has better conversations with his direct reports about the key things that need to get done to grow the company and make money.

No one lives in a vacuum, and neither should a small business. External data is often as important as internal information and insights. The most obvious way to gain quick access to at least rudimentary data is to conduct online research. SMBs have a wealth of information about their competitors, their industry, and potential employees at their fingertips and don't need to pay exorbitant amounts for consultants or experts. Trade associations are a great source for relevant information, but the internet is still the cheapest, fastest, and most reliable way to learn a lot.

There is another good way to understand quickly what's going on within a business as well as in the outside world without a lot of data or systems. It's also something that most leaders of SMBs don't take enough advantage of: talking to their employees. Unfortunately, the need to look good or acting on unfounded fears about what they may hear sometimes gets in the way of this very simple act. When these fears or mindsets overwhelm a leader, he or she often finds it difficult and demotivating to go to the team yet again and discuss issues. Energy goes down, and the problem just gets worse. Many leaders begin to suspect their team is not very good, which just exacerbates the situation.

Conversations should be the core of any small business leader's toolbox. They're the way we stay in touch, build bonds, exchange ideas, sort out plans, fix problems, and take action. Communication or the lack of it is a constant complaint in most teams—and at the bottom of better communication is an ability to have better conversations.

Better conversation also means better teamwork. The way teams talk with each other is a telling indicator of the level of morale, culture, climate, performance, and team cohesion. It's a key element in the effective functioning of any team. Yet while we engage in conversations all the time, the importance of becoming more skilled at conversations seems to escape us. Many of us work together for years and never take the time to reflect on how we come across or talk to each other.

And the first step to having meaningful conversations is to ask good questions.

SECTION 14

The Questioning Leader

Earlier I explained that questions are at the heart of my practice. Questions give me the permission to go to many places with my clients. Only when I have a deep understanding of their goals and ambitions, the current state of their business and how they process information and make decisions can I help them develop practical solutions to issues and problems unique to their situation. I'm also in a much better position to focus on the areas they need to develop to become better leaders and disruptors.

But there's another reason why questions are so integral to what I do. Most leaders are uncomfortable asking their employees questions— they often feel it makes them look weaker. I've learned that it has quite the opposite effect. The ability to ask good questions actually makes them better leaders in the eyes of those with whom they work. Thus, my methodology is also designed to help clients recognize the value of asking the right questions.

There are a lot of not-so-interesting or downright demotivating leaders who simply don't know when to stop the gush of words emanating from their mouths. Some senior executives simply like thinking out loud, while others get so energized that they literally can't shut up. Many honestly just love the sound of their own voice. More than a few aren't really that interested in what other people have to say, anyway.

Everyone has probably worked for a verbose leader at one time or another. These kinds of executives often spend a lot of time telling people how to do their jobs. Sometimes they're so enthralled with their own vision that they don't want to let anyone or anything get in their way— certainly not employees who might only have a "limited" understanding of the situation or personal agendas they're pursuing.

They wonder why there is so little initiative, team spirit, and entrepreneurial drive in their organizations. They get furious when the same problem they think they've fixed occurs over and over again. Communication in their organizations rapidly deteriorates, and their ability to get underneath the business and understand what's really happening can become almost impossible. Their businesses frequently head south quickly.

That's generally around the time they start thinking about hiring consultants to solve the problem.

What these executives probably don't know is that even in the best of situations, most people only take in about 30 percent of what they are told. Frequently, whatever they tell their employees—regardless of how developed their communication skills are—is forgotten quickly and not acted upon.

But when these same employees are asked probing questions first and put into a position of having to think and come up with an answer themselves, quite the opposite happens. People in these situations remember almost 70 percent of the conversation. Because they own the answer and the activities required to implement the solution they arrived at, they are more motivated to follow through. Accountability automatically goes up.

So why don't more leaders take advantage of this powerful tool?

First, there's always the danger of finding out things a senior executive might not want to hear about himself, his team, or the broader organization. Second, many executives are so caught up in the day-to-day worries of meeting payroll, serving clients and customers, and trying to grow their businesses that they easily lapse into a command-and-control mentality. Asking well-formulated, thoughtful questions at just the right time can be difficult and requires more time than simply providing the answer.

But more importantly, too many executives are afraid that if they don't have all the answers, they'll be taken less seriously as leaders, and that makes them vulnerable. Worst case, they're afraid that asking too many questions might make them look like they don't know what they're doing.

Indeed, there are situations in business that call for a more command-and-control leadership, such as major crises or when there is short turnaround time for something to be completed.

There are many reasons why this is a great technique for increasing the effectiveness of a senior executive and his or her staff:

1. Asking questions minimizes the chance of misinterpretation. If done properly, employees will be motivated to understand the actions they should take and feel more at ease asking clarifying questions.

2. Leaders with good questioning skills are better able to gather information more quickly and more completely than their less-skilled counterparts. They often find themselves one step ahead of everyone else, which in turn helps them be better leaders.

3. The simple act of asking someone a sincere question or soliciting an opinion breaks down barriers to communication that inevitably arise between a senior executive and employees. Good questions show you care.

4. Questions are also a great way to diffuse difficult situations. Instead of issuing commands that might not pierce through the tension of a given moment, a questioning leader can change the dynamic in a split second by stepping away and asking a good question.

But there's another, less well-understood advantage to asking great questions, especially for all of us control freaks out there. Consider for a moment that the person asking the questions has much more control of the conversation than the person (or persons) being asked. The questioner is in a better position to steer the conversation anywhere he or she wants it to go, while the other party has little choice than to follow along. It's a far more advanced and subtler form of control than barking out orders.

But all of this requires the questioner also to be a good listener and observer.

SECTION 15

You and Your Decisions

The exercise below is a good way to understand your current preferences when making decisions while highlighting what you need to improve: gut, judgment and perspectives. It can also be used to understand how you make personal decisions and to assess your leadership team and managers.

1. Put together a list of decisions you've made over the past few years. It doesn't matter how mission-critical you think those decisions were; they just need to be decisions you were personally responsible for, regardless of who else provided input.

   Did you make a decision about how you reward and promote employees at your company? Write it down. Did you add new products or services to your company's portfolio? Put those individual decisions on the list. Did you sign a lease for new office space? Did you start a major marketing initiative? Add those all to your list.

2. Now rank-order them, starting with the decision you feel had the greatest impact on your business at the top of the list, down to the least impactful. Then indicate next to each decision how you made them:

   • I made the decision using minimal or no input or hard data, preferring instead to rely on my experience and knowledge (i.e., gut feelings/instincts).

   • I did a little fact-checking, called some knowledgeable friends or experts, and/or talked to my team just to be sure (i.e., judgment).

- I tried to be as fact-based as possible, relying almost exclusively on the data my team or I could get our hands on (i.e., perspectives).

3. Assuming you know the outcomes of these decisions, rate the relative success of each decision on a scale from one to ten to the right of each item. "One" represents "the worst decision I've ever made, and it cost my team and me a lot financially, personally, and/or legally." "Ten" is "I knocked the ball out of the park."

You'll likely discover some important things when you review the results of this exercise, including:

- The relative importance of using data or your gut instinct when making your best decisions versus your not-so-successful decisions
- Whether you were better at making the big, important decisions or the small, relatively unimportant ones

4. You'll remember from section eleven that there are three other factors that influence the way we make decisions: the element of time (e.g., urgency), complexity and the degree of uncertainty related to outcomes. Go back and repeat step two by ranking the decisions on your list again, but this time according to each of these three other criteria. That will help you understand the extent to which these other factors influenced how you made those decision.

Maybe you have never or rarely use data to make decisions, and after doing the exercise, you wish you had more than gut instinct to go on. You very well might need to start at the beginning of gathering data—join your industry's trade association, take the time to search topics yourself or with someone's assistance, and talk with your team or people you know and trust.

It could also be that you can find good external data, but you have the same problem as Salomon, and you either have systems that don't produce the reports you need, or the format confuses you more than it helps. In the first case, you should find a good IT systems company or solo practitioner to fix the problem. In the second, you should work with the person who delivers the reports or a coach to help you understand what the data means and how you can use it to make better decisions. Maybe you need to make changes to the format or content to fit your needs.

You might discover that you don't ask enough probing questions. Maybe it's out of a sense of decorum, or a fear of appearing too aggressive or inappropriate. Maybe you've convinced yourself that by asking questions you look weak or uninformed. With some self-awareness or coaching you'll learn to identify these beliefs and even learn how to not let them get in the way of constructive Q&A. But for those of you who think you know all the answers or that no one knows your business better than you, the path to better leadership of any kind will be tough.

Most likely you will have to work hard and use a lot of self-discipline to stop yourself at moments in key conversations and ask a question, or maybe even a whole series of questions. Once you see how much this helps, you'll begin feeling increasingly comfortable in the role of someone seeking advice. You will understand that asking questions is not a vulnerability, but a sign of good leadership.

In addition, think about decisions you should have made but didn't. Maybe you put off a decision, simply ignored it, or delegated it to someone else in the organization. Maybe you were overwhelmed by too much information and/or spent too much time seeking everybody's opinion and as many data points as you could find. It's entirely possible you get stuck in endless loops of "analysis paralysis," and your organization is hurting because of that. If that's the case, you may have not addressed some of the fears from the previous section.

Go to **www.JohnFFurth.com/worksheets** to download the template "You and Your Decisions." Using this together with the process described above will give you a comprehensive view of how you make decisions and what you could improve.

PART FOUR

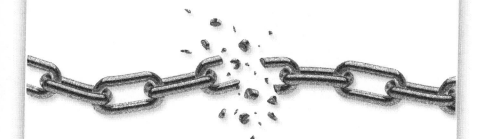

IS YOUR BUSINESS A PLANNING AND EXECUTION MACHINE?

SECTION 16

If You Don't Know Where You're Going, Any Path Will Take You There

T he single most important activity that a company needs to perfect in order to grow is the annual exercise we call Strategic Planning. It helps a CEO and his or her leadership team think through, plan and execute major growth initiatives and investments.

It is, however, not something that most people have a natural talent for. In fact, I've discovered that without proper guidance many young CEOs don't take it very seriously. Their natural tendency is to fall into one of two mindsets:

The Creative Visionaries: These leaders enjoy the creative, analytical, and forward-thinking activities of the business. Unfortunately, these types get easily bored by the details of implementation and/or make such sudden shifts in direction that nothing can ever get fully implemented.

Sean, the dreamer in my Vistage group, was very much of this mindset at first. He used to spend whole days planning and plotting the future while leaving the all-important implementation to his team without really making them accountable. After a while, he would forget what he had asked them to do, which in turn made his team less motivated to complete any strategies they thought they had agreed to. Sean is very lucky that even after two years, his new president, Jeremy, provides a perfect counterweight as someone who is obsessive about good execution.

The Doers: On the other hand, there are those business owners who are so obsessed with the day-to-day operations of their companies that they can't plan more than a few days ahead. Alan, a wholesaler of auto tires, is a perfect example of a doer who refuses to look more than a few days out. He is not at all a proponent of what he considers to be purely abstract thinking. Until we began working together, he and his company were stuck in a version of the *Groundhog Day* loop where nothing ever changed and growth was elusive and unattainable.

Without a good strategic planning process, there is a high cost to an organization when senior executives start moving in different directions on separate agendas. Missed opportunities or increased confusion can destroy a young company faster than anything I know.

When an organization and its leaders can both plan strategically *and* execute well, a virtuous circle begins:

1. The company's leadership is always working toward a mutually agreed vision.

2. This team is fully committed and passionate about executing a laser-focused action plan.

3. Everyone buys into goals that are crystal clear, motivating, and time-bound.

4. Specific people who will reliably execute tasks are paired with deadlines for completion of critical steps.

A good strategic planning process also strengthens the all-important system of accountability which is used to measure people's performance. This is key for rewarding high performers and identifying and removing nonperformers.

There are some gifted young leaders who can both formulate and communicate a compelling vision and a three-year strategic plan *while also* being able to lead consistent but agile and flexible implementation of its activities. Most aspiring leaders need to take the plunge and learn how to do both well.

A strategic planning process typically begins during the summer and finishes around October or November before the new year begins, assuming that is also the start of a company's fiscal year. The output of such a strategic plan should be a clearly defined implementation roadmap with accountabilities for the coming year. But even then, a one-year plan means very little to the organization if the leader doesn't have a longer-term strategic vision for at least the next three years.

Paradoxically, once leaders grasp how effective good strategic planning and execution can be, they can often turn around 180 degrees and believe this is the magic bullet they've been looking for. The reality is, even with a clearly defined implementation plan, in this disruptive world things change quickly and without notice. An agile organization makes appropriate changes to the plan quickly so the company can grow properly and take advantages of opportunities or avoid pitfalls as they present themselves.

Analyzing and developing a deep understanding of the data an organization gathers is vital to the success of a strategic planning process. An easy-to-understand and practical tool for most organizations is a SWOT analysis. SWOT stands for strengths, weaknesses, opportunities, and threats, per the example below.

SWOT Analyis for Software Developent Company

Strengths	Weaknesses
1. Excellent working relationship with partners	1. Young and inexperienced management team
2. Hard working and highly motivated team	2. Many unstructured or nonexistent processes
3. Diverse backgrounds and industry expertise	3. Resource constrained (especially staff) and small margin for error
4. Great entrepreneurial culture with opportunities for individuals to grow and take on responsibility	4. Little or no external marketing
Opportunities	**Threats**
1. Many possibilities to grow and expand business	1. Potential mass exodus of delivery staff due to unhappiness and/or being overworked
2. Better recruitment of delivery staff using new recruiter and referrals from employees	2. Poor implementation and negative customer experience could possibly lead to being blacklisted by partners
3. Better utilization of delivery staff to improve bottom line and reduce wear and tear	3. Competition (low barriers to entry)
4. Increased use of offshore teams	4. Aggressive growth without profitability

A good SWOT analysis touches on everything a company does to operate well: marketing, sales, operations, finance, HR, and so on. For this reason, all members of a strategic planning team should fill one out prior to a planning retreat and submit it to the facilitator, who then aggregates the results. If completed correctly, this tool can get even some of the most buried and complicated problems out in the open and should hopefully answer many key questions:

- How well does the organization handle competitive threats and external forces in terms of its competition and customers? What can the organization do to better handle those competitive threats?

- Is the company positioned for growth in terms of its products, services, and markets served? What changes to the company's products and services and/or its customer base would better achieve its goals? What new markets, products, and services should the company pursue?

- How strong are the organization's people, financials, marketing, and sales? Is the company hiring, developing, and retaining the best talent at a price it can afford?

- Does the company have the financial resources and the ability to take on certain risks that will clearly result in improvements to the top and bottom lines?

Many other kinds of analyses are used to make sense of large amounts of data and add value to a strategic planning exercise. One of my favorites is the Boston Consulting Group (BCG) Matrix, which can bring focus to an otherwise difficult discussion about the past, present, and potential future performance of a company's product portfolio.

The BCG Matrix is made up of four quadrants, per below. Developed about fifty years ago, you'll notice how the names given to the four quadrants have become part of everyday business parlance.

BCG Matrix

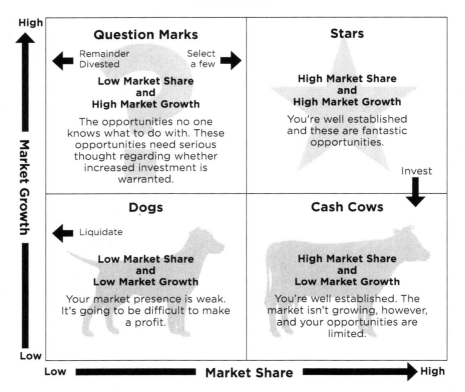

The X-axis represents the share a company's products and/or services have of their respective markets at the time of the analysis. The Y-axis is the growth rate of those markets over a period of time, usually three or five years. (Depending on the reliability of the data, that growth rate can also be projected out several years into the future.)

In the top right-hand corner are a company's star products and service lines that have dominant positions in high-growth markets. Sometimes these products are the result of a particularly disruptive event by a company that either reinvigorates an existing market or creates a whole new segment. Companies need to ensure that star products retain their leadership position for a long time by making smart investments in product development and marketing.

A company's cash cows are represented by the lower right-hand quadrant. Like stars, these products and/or services dominate their markets. The difference, however, is that their markets are growing slower and are not as attractive as those of a company's stars. Competitive threats to a dominant position are therefore less likely. Cash cows require less maintenance than stars, but under no circumstances should their existence become compromised without considerable analysis and thought.

In the upper left-hand quadrant are the question marks—i.e., those products and/or services that command a low share of high-growth markets. These tend to be recent investments in markets that a company has entered later than others. These can be markets dominated by a few big players or where development and innovation occur rapidly. Maybe the company reviewing its portfolio is trying to displace current players. For these reasons and others, the future is not always obvious. A company's leadership needs to constantly assess the extent to which they want to dedicate valuable resources to this part of the portfolio.

In the lower left-hand corner are a company's dogs, which are marginal products and services in stagnant markets. Leaders who allow issues other than the long-term health of their business to sway their judgment—such as internal politics or short-term financial concerns—often hold onto these businesses until it's too late. The best leaders, however, take decisive action to sell off or close down these low performers.

The BCG Matrix was meant to be used by large companies with complex portfolios of products and services. Such companies command significant shares of large markets that can be monitored and tracked using readily available information. Unfortunately, most SMBs are active in niche markets or product segments, and/or the percentage share their products and services command in their markets is just too small to track. This makes it difficult for many SMBs to use the BCG Matrix effectively.

I have developed a few alternatives that can be useful if, for example, internal financials are the only reliable data available. In most cases, however, some assessment of the marketplace must be included in the discussion, even if it is only anecdotal and qualitative.

Repurposed BCG Chart for Analyzing Product/Business Portfolios of SMBs

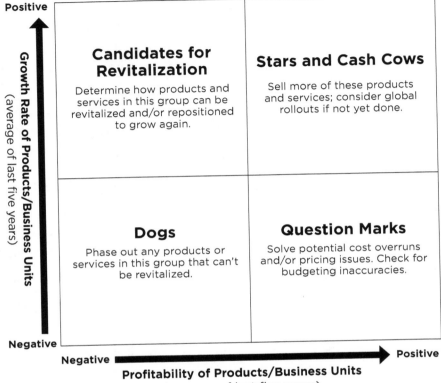

There are additional ways financial data can be parsed and analyzed to gain valuable insights for a strategic planning session. As long as the information they have is reliable, most CFOs and their teams are able to calculate return on investment (ROI) or the net present value (NPV) of possible investments. This work provides necessary insights to help senior management make the right choices from among a variety of options competing for a small pool of financial resources.

In section thirteen, I talked about working with my client Salomon and his leadership team to develop a simple but powerful monthly financial report for his company. Among many other benefits, these reports finally made it possible for Salomon's finance administrator, Joel, to easily and thoroughly analyze which options discussed in the strategy sessions would provide the company with the best ROI in the short term. With this clarity we realized we had made some decisions in earlier meetings that would have been less beneficial and even in some cases would have worsened the company's perilous financial position. Those decisions were reversed immediately.

I am often asked to develop insights using many sources of data to make a strategic planning session more meaningful and drive better decisions. Inevitably, the most important source of insights are interviews with customers. Most of my clients are understandably nervous about the kind of feedback they might receive and naturally default to asking me to talk to only their most loyal and happiest customers.

Once they understand, however, that this is not an exercise in customer loyalty but rather a discovery process to determine what needs to change or be optimized, they calm down about the prospect of my talking to customers no longer working with them. Insights from former customers about the quality of my clients' products and services and, more importantly, about other companies they are served by (i.e., my clients' competitors) often prove more valuable than input from happy clients.

In the long run, the level of a strategic planning team's creativity and desire to get to the root cause of a company's issues will determine the quality of the analytic tools that are developed and then used.

SECTION 17

Running a Successful Strategic Planning Meeting

I t's best to hold a strategic planning session off-site, away from distractions, and working through the process face-to-face until the plan is complete. That creates an environment for:

- A full and confidential airing of sensitive issues away from employees

- In-person debate with no one hiding behind emails, texts, or phone calls

- Important bonding between the members of an organization's leadership team

It is important that the CEO be a participant in the retreat but not the leader. To ensure commitment, strategic planning team members must have the feeling the CEO is driving them to create a combined plan, not his or her plan. For this reason, hiring a facilitator is recommended, so the CEO is not compromised.

When using a facilitator, make sure it is an outsider to the organization with no emotional investment in the outcomes. Prior to the retreat, the facilitator should meet with each planning team member, ideally in person. The purpose of these meetings is to get acquainted, explain the retreat format, and hear each team member's desired outcomes.

Although a typical planning retreat lasts about two full days, I have handled it in different ways, depending on a client's specific needs, availability, and degree of knowledge and experience with such sessions. Contrast two different approaches: one "light" (the process only really involved two primary decision-makers) and one that requires a lot of buy-in from many stakeholders and thus is by necessity far more complex.

Approach One. Sean was eager to use a strategic planning session to get himself aligned with Jeremy, whom he had just promoted to president of his company. I asked Sean and Jeremy to gather as much internal financial and client information as they could to prepare for a one-day session in September. I pointed out that the data itself was not as important as the insights they were able to gain by working through it together.

Sean rented a meeting room at his country club just outside New York City. It took about three hours for us to come to a common understanding of the company's current situation. After lunch, we developed solutions to the thorniest issues of market positioning and client engagement, the output of which has been discussed earlier in this book. The session was successful in that it helped Sean and Jeremy find common ground to work together more seamlessly.

They then went behind closed doors for a few weeks to hammer out separate implementation plans for both of them—Sean in charge of sales and marketing, Jeremy handling project delivery and operational issues. I joined them for two sessions of two hours each to review these plans.

Approach Two. I'm often asked to perform one-off strategy projects. While typical clients are small companies, these organizations usually have never taken a hard look at themselves, their customers, or their competitors, and want to do a full 360-degree assessment. I consider such assignments to be strategic planning projects, except that they require far more up-front research and planning.

A typical project lasts approximately three months and involves the following components:

- *External market assessments*, which include interviews with twenty-five to thirty current, former, and potential clients, internet research on leading competitors, key markets, and trends.

- *Internal reviews* with a company's leadership team, reviewing lists of targeted clients and marketing materials (e.g., ads, intellectual capital, etc.) developed over the last three to five years is a very important exercise. I also ask clients to provide me with the key metrics they track at the time of the project, such as percent of new clients versus existing clients, marketing and business development spending, etc.

Usually, my team and I will need two or three long conference calls with a company's leadership team to prepare them for the session.

A typical session covers the following points:

1. Share all analyses and invite commentary. By the end, the team should agree what the key learnings and take-aways are.

2. Create the future three-year strategic vision. This addresses the crucial elements of what the company will look like in three years—what products/services and target clients should be developed, geographic markets addressed, most important strategic initiatives to be completed, as well as behaviors and core values which employees should be hired and developed against.

3. Determine three-year financial goals. These should be clearly tied to the strategic vision.

SECTION 18

Clear Accountability = Successful Execution

Once you have finished the strategic part of the retreat agenda, the next steps are to plan the key initiatives of the coming year. The implementation plan must include a chart for each initiative and address:

- The clearly articulated goal
- The champion or ultimate person responsible for completing the entire initiative
- Specific action steps
- Who (by name) is responsible for each action step and who will hold these people accountable for their individual action steps
- The action step deadline shown as month and date
- A column for the results

If you leave a retreat and never revisit the written plan again as a group, you have wasted time and money. *Thus, it is important that you conduct eleven monthly accountability meetings to check up on progress toward the achievement of action items.* In these meetings, the written plan should be reviewed goal by goal, updating and changing it as you go, wherever the team agrees. These meetings can by facilitated by the CEO, an outside consultant, or for a creative and empowering twist, rotate facilitation duties among all team members.

Implementation of the plan can run aground unless it's determined what will happen to nonperformers. Lackluster performance and missed deadlines without prior notification or a legitimate reason for why they were missed need to have consequences. No one has the individual right to change the plan without a group decision. It's tough love with prudent allowances made for unexpected crisis situations. Do not create consequences if you aren't going to enforce the disciplinary steps the group agrees on; it will do more harm than good.

I saw first-hand how even the best planning efforts can fall apart without preparing and agreeing to a detailed implementation plan when I was working with a consulting company that specializes in leadership development and team management. The partner in charge of the program was a very smart, Harvard-educated woman. She was duty-bound to get at the heart of why the company was growing so poorly. I was given a research assistant to help me, and for three months conducted analyses on the organization's key competitors, the markets it was currently serving in terms of industries and geographies, and potential new markets it should go after.

It was a satisfying intellectual pursuit and the leadership team was impressed and happy with the results. However, we finished the day's strategic planning retreat without spending one second on developing an implementation plan for accountability. I occasionally circled back with them, but several partners left and I don't think the growth that they had hoped for ever took place.

Because accountability is the only way to ensure proper execution, it plays a large role in my practice.

The members of my Vistage group process a lot of issues when the group meets or in their individual sessions. Every issue should start with the question, "How do I (do something)?" The issues must be urgent and important, whether it is firing an unproductive employee, rolling out a new product or service, making an important hire, having a difficult conversation with a customer or employee, implementing a new IT or financial system, and so on.

This process is by nature discovery-oriented and no one is entirely sure where the group will land. It is question-based, and only when the issue is really understood do members of the group start offering solutions.

The person who asked the question then chooses the solution that he or she feels could work best. The two or three most important steps that a member or client needs to take to get an initiative underway, as well as dates of completion are agreed to, and become the member's accountabilities.

No group meeting goes by without first checking on everyone's accountabilities. If someone is behind, they have to explain to the entire group why that happened and whether there is a fundamental change in their plans or whether they simply got distracted.

If executed correctly, such meetings exert pressure on the members of the group to perform. No one in the group wants to be the person who agrees to something and can't implement it. It's also fruitless to lie, as it will always come out later when something goes wrong at their company and can be traced back to nonperformance. This lets members experience what it means to be held accountable and how powerful it is.

(A word to the wise: There is always a certain amount of flexibility required during implementation. Market and economic situations as well as a company's financial position can change quickly. In a period of great disruption, this need to manage flexibility becomes even more important. We'll explore this issue more in section thirty-three.)

SECTION 19

Commit to Your Path and Run with It

Te strategic planning and implementation process is a method to gain commitment on important initiatives that move a company forward. Without good strategic planning and implementation, an organization gets into trouble quickly or can't solve basic problems that creep up on it. Luck can carry a leader and his team just so far.

Here is a simple distillation of this part in an easy-to-understand, step-by-step guide to get started. If you are already using a planning and implementation process in your company or elsewhere, it will still behoove you to compare your process against this checklist.

1. Hire a facilitator or consultant who has run these sorts of processes before. Prepare and refine a system that will work for you and your leadership team. Plan the dates for the off-site meeting and pick the members of the team—ideally covering all the important functional areas—who will be involved. Define the external and internal data you will need, how you will get it, and how it should be analyzed and presented.

2. Working with your facilitator, have your strategic planning team gather the data and prepare it as agreed to. The facilitator should not only run any external client, customer, or expert interviews, but also hold regular update calls with the strategic planning team to help them prepare for the meeting. Flexibility during this discovery phase is very important.

3. Prepare the workshop agenda and determine the roles you and your team will play.

4. Run the off-site meeting using the guidelines above and make sure all decisions are documented. Prepare the year's implementation plans accordingly, with clearly defined accountabilities, due dates, etc. Make sure it is clear what consequences nonperformance will have.

5. Communicate important decisions, such as the three-year vision or financials, to the entire company as appropriate.

6. Hold monthly implementation meetings to track the ongoing implementation of the most important initiatives. Make changes as necessary, but reward excellent performance and take the necessary actions with nonperformers.

Go to **www.JohnFFurth.com/worksheets**
to download sample agendas for strategic
planning meetings.

PART FIVE

THE POWER
OF INTERNAL
DISRUPTIONS

SECTION 20

If It Can Happen at Big Blue, It Can Happen to You

By the early 1990s, IBM had become a bloated organization of some 400,000 employees. It had invested heavily in a myriad of low-margin, transactional, commodity businesses. Technologies IBM had invented and or commercialized—DRAM, hard disk drives, the PC, electric typewriters—were no longer competitive. The company had a massive international organization characterized by redundant processes and functions, and its cost structure couldn't compete with smaller, less diversified competitors.

But it was the back-to-back revolutions of the PC and the client server that dramatically undermined IBM's core mainframe business and forced IBM into a tailspin. Both revolutions transformed the way customers viewed, used, and bought technology. Companies' purchasing decisions were placed in the hands of individuals and departments—not the places where IBM had long-standing customer relationships.

Piece-part technologies took precedence over integrated solutions. The focus was now on the desktop and personal productivity, not on business applications across the enterprise. As a result, IBM's earnings—which had been at or above $5 billion since the early 1980s—dropped by more than a third, to $3 billion in 1989. A brief spike in earnings in 1990 proved illusory as corporate spending continued to shift from high-profit-margin mainframes to lower-margin, microprocessor-based systems.

John Akers, IBM's CEO at the time, tried to stop the bleeding through a variety of initiatives. But these efforts failed to halt the slide. After two consecutive years of losses of more than $1 billion, on January 19, 1993,

IBM announced an $8 billion loss for the 1992 financial year, which at the time was the largest single-year corporate loss in United States history.

IBM's board knew something had to change dramatically. But they also understood this was less about developing and implementing a grand design to disrupt the IT industry or unseat major competitors and more about applying a series of disruptive shocks to IBM's business model, strategy, internal systems, and culture to save it. In any case, it was not going to be easy and the risks of failure were very high.

The board's first step after firing John Akers was probably one of the most disruptive actions ever undertaken by a board of directors in the history of American business. They hired a CEO who had never run a high-tech company before—large or small—and was by his own admission almost technology-phobic. That man was Lou Gerstner.

But Gerstner brought other highly relevant skills and experiences. He was an engineer by training and had the pedigree of a Harvard Business School education and a stint at McKinsey. After that, he had risen through the ranks at American Express to become its CEO, after which he was tapped to run Nabisco.

But Gerstner's greatest asset was having the mindset of the consumer of IBM products and not an IBM manager.

When Gerstner arrived at the company in April 1993, the prevailing wisdom was that the company's core mainframe business was headed for obsolescence. IBM's own management was in the process of allowing its various divisions—the so-called "Baby Blues"—to rebrand and manage themselves. Akers had decided that the logical and rational solution was to split IBM into autonomous business units (such as processors, storage, software, services, printers) that he reasoned could stand up to IBM's competitors, which were more focused and agile and had lower cost structures.

Gerstner knew from his previous roles that the biggest problem all major companies faced in 1993 was integrating all the separate computing technologies that were emerging at the time. He realized that IBM's unique competitive advantage was its ability to provide integrated solutions for customers—a company that could represent more than piece parts or components. Like all great disruptors, Gerstner literally forced IBM to become a customer-centric company.

He quickly jettisoned the widely held view that IBM should be broken up into smaller pieces. His choice to keep the company together gave IBM the capabilities to deliver complete IT solutions to customers. Services could be sold as an add-on to companies that had already bought IBM computers. Barely profitable pieces of hardware were used to open the door to more profitable deals.

Akers, a company lifer, had been excessively immersed in the company's culture. Remaining loyal to traditional ways had blinded him to the grim realities of the situation. As an outsider, Gerstner had no emotional attachment to the lackluster products IBM had developed to try to regain control of the PC market. For example, Gerstner saw that in spite of OS/2's technical superiority to the dominant Microsoft Windows 3.0, his colleagues were unwilling or unable to accept they had suffered a resounding defeat. It "was draining tens of millions of dollars, absorbing huge chunks of senior management's time, and making a mockery of our image."[11] By the end of 1994, IBM ceased new development of OS/2 software and in 2012, IBM withdrew from the retail desktop PC market entirely, which had become unprofitable due to price pressures in the early 2000s.

As with many successful disruptions, there was also a lot of short-term misery. Gerstner laid off more than 100,000 employees which in short order killed one of IBM's holiest cows: the promise of lifetime employment. Because IBM employees were generally rewarded based on seniority and not performance, the majority had grown lax.[12] This was a dangerous situation which in turn angered and demoralized top-performers at the company.

---

[11] Gerstner, Louis V. *Who Says Elephants Can't Dance? Leading a Great Enterprise through Dramatic Change.* New York, NY: HarperBusiness, 2003.

[12] Berger, Joseph. "The Pain of Layoffs for Ex-Senior I.B.M. Workers; In Dutchess County, a Disorienting Time for Employees Less Hardened to Job Loss." *The New York Times.* December 21, 1993. http://www.nytimes.com/1993/12/22/nyregion/pain-layoffs-for-ex-senior-ibm-workers-dutchess-county-disorienting-time-for.html.

Gerstner's disruption of IBM was a resounding success, at least for a few years. From 1993 until Gerstner's retirement in 2002, IBM's market capitalization rose from $29 billion to $168 billion. By the end of the 1990s, however, IBM had ceded its once-dominant position in the IT industry to other, more disruptive organizations such as Microsoft, Apple, and Dell. At the same time, Google emerged and created new computer-based business empires.

In his published writing about the success he had at IBM, Gerstner never once uses the term "disruption" to describe what he did. One reason was because the development of the management science now called "disruptive management" had not yet really begun in earnest. At the time, professors and practitioners used terms such as "turnaround management," "change management," etc.

It wasn't until 1997—three years after Gerstner's disruption of IBM started—that Clay Christensen published his first book, *The Innovator's Dilemma*. This book laid the foundation for much of his and other academics' research and teaching on the subject. This book also marked the beginning of the broader business community's awareness of the power of disruption.

Comparing Internal and External Disruptions

There are, of course, major differences between the kind of big, external disruptions practiced by Amazon and the more internal-facing disruptions implemented by Gerstner at IBM. Certainly Amazonian-style disruptions have the power to transform the lives of millions of people, whereas smaller, internal disruptions generally only affect those directly involved with the organization being disrupted. Bigger, market-shaping disruptions are about unlocking value within an ecosystem by changing the rules of the game. But because there are so many unknown variables, it's very difficult for a leader and his team to truly understand the effects of these kinds of disruptions until quite late in the process. Internal disruptions, on the other hand, are about carefully rebuilding value that an organization has lost and are very specific. Thus, they can (and have to be) planned out in far more detail.

The fact is that internal disruptions can be as psychologically, intellectually, and physically exhausting as the larger variety, if not more so. They often require just as much courage, insight, and hard work from a CEO and his or her team as the momentous, history-changing, big disruptions. Both kinds of disruptions require leaders, their teams, or their advisers to have the ability and insight to recognize a problem that can only be solved through some sort of disruptive event and then act on that.

There is another major reason why IBM's internally-driven disruptions might be considered smaller than Amazon's, given the relatively fewer number of people directly affected by the initiatives. IBM is a business-to-business (B2B) company. This automatically caps the size of the community the company and its employees will ever be able to directly touch. By comparison, as a business-to-consumer (B2C) company, Amazon's potentially addressable market is very large—basically everyone on the planet.

B2B companies generally have long-term contracts for services and products from their vendors, and product innovation and introduction often takes many years. Business customers consider other factors when deciding on a service or product provider, especially in a competitive marketplace. These include quality, cost, responsiveness, knowledge of the customer's industry, and reliability.

Gerstner was not a "product person," at least not when it came to new technologies. He was an organization expert, and that's ultimately what he was hired to do—shake IBM to its core by addressing organizational issues that had grossly hindered IBM from formulating and delivering value to its customers. Once IBM's customers saw a difference in how the company was performing, growth and success were not far behind.

B2C companies, by contrast, are more often than not evaluated solely on basis of the actual products and/or services they offer. Thus, innovation and time-to-market are the most important attributes of delivering on a value proposition. Consumers often purchase impulsively or on a try-it-and-see-if-I-like-it basis. The only really sustainable revenue models are memberships and subscriptions, but these are often very easy to cancel and/or not renew.

Amazon, like many other B2C companies, needs to be highly innovative and fast to market with constantly new and updated products and services. However, as Amazon grows and begins entering traditional B2B markets, the complexity of the organization will increasingly require Bezos and his team to disrupt their organization as Gerstner did with IBM to continue delivering on its promises.

The chart below highlights the differences between some of the internal disruptions during the first few years of Gerstner's leadership of IBM and Amazon's bigger, more external disruptions.

Amazon

Disruptive Event (Product)	Short-Term Negative Impact	Long-Term Positive Impact	Approximate Number of People Directly Affected
Kindle e-Reader	Positioned to further weaken Amazon's main competitor, Barnes & Noble, and their e-reader, the Nook	Now the number one e-reader in the world, the Kindle's inexpensive design ensures Amazon can sell it at a cost that is affordable to billions of people. It both relies on and supports Amazon's ecosystem, while fulfilling the company's mission.	Hundreds of millions of readers in the world as well as Amazon's main competitors
Amazon Web Services	None	AWS is a cash cow for Amazon. By pricing its cloud products extremely competitively, Amazon can provide affordable and scalable services to everyone, from the smallest start-up to a Fortune 500 company.	Hundreds of millions of business leaders and leading technology providers
Amazon Home Services	Could potentially put a lot of start-ups in this sector out of business; loss of independence for many repair people and other small service providers	Amazon can offer affordable and reliable services for consumers around the world.	Potentially billions of people
Amazon Go grocery stores	Could potentially affect millions of grocery store operators and fast moving consumer goods (FMCG) manufacturers	Amazon offers faster checkout and better merchandising through its advanced technology.	Millions of grocery store operators and FMCG manufacturers in the world

IBM

Disruptive Event (Product)	Short-Term Negative Impact	Long-Term Positive Impact	Approximate Number of People Directly Affected
Slashing of IBM's pension fund	Loss of competitiveness when hiring new talent and a demoralized employee base	IBM increased cash flow to fund operations and R&D	IBM's entire workforce except for the most senior executives
Termination of approx. 25 percent of IBM's workforce	Approximately 100,000 employees laid off; many went on to find new opportunities, but some never restored their careers	The message was clear that the IBM of old was gone. A massive one-time layoff reduced the uncertainty and politically charged atmosphere caused by the fear of possible additional layoffs. There was a rise in organizational productivity.	Close to 200,000 IBM employees— not only those who were laid off, but also those who stayed and worked with Gerstner's team to rebuild IBM
Requirement that IBM's business unit heads present just one-page summaries at business review meetings	Business Unit heads were partially thrown into confusion as to what exactly was expected of them.	Senior executives focused far more on the important things that would move IBM forward; time wasted preparing for and attending business reviews was decreased significantly.	Approximately 200 senior executives as well as their direct reports
"Normalization" of IBM's traditional dress code	Employee confusion	An organization more in line with modern standards made it more attractive as an employer of choice.	The entire IBM workforce

SECTION 22

No Disruption is Too Small

Not every entrepreneur wants to build the next big company by disrupting an entire industry. But even if many entrepreneurs and their employees are happy staying small and flexible, the capability to disrupt themselves and/or their competitors is often the only way to stay in business. Because of the limited resources available to them, SMBs can become quickly destabilized by even just one poorly performing employee, an aggressive local competitor, changing regulations, and other ostensibly minor circumstances.

Unfortunately, many CEOs of outwardly successful SMBs downplay the need for these small disruptions out of fear of destroying what they have built or preferring to go into stealth mode until they are more confident. Others become hamstrung to the point that they can clearly see disaster looming on the horizon and yet do nothing for years until it's too late.

But even the most successful CEOs and their teams can become complacent if they don't watch out. Some get so overwhelmed by the day-to-day demands of operating their companies that they resist any disruption because of the uncertainty and risk that comes with such an endeavor. Many leaders develop blind spots that make it virtually impossible to know when and how to disrupt aspects of their businesses that are no longer working. Most don't even know what disruption is and how powerful it can be when done right.

When I met my client Alan, he was running the company he had founded fifty-one years earlier, selling tires just-in-time to local garages for same-day automotive repairs. While his ability to sustain a company for so long was admirable, the fear of losing everything just before he retired made it difficult for him to justify making any significant investments or changes. The irony, of course, was that his unwillingness to disrupt himself, his company, and his competitors almost put him out of business.

Alan had watched as his local competitors were bought up by larger enterprises over the years. He knew that these increasingly large companies had the capital to invest more in new technology and people as well as the purchasing power to demand lower prices from the leading tire manufacturers. At the same time, he had allowed his organization to grow weeds by not letting poorly performing employees go and by hiring people who may have been affordable for a company working with tight margins, but who often turned out to be highly problematic.

Alan's girlfriend, Rhonda, clearly understood what was going on and pushed him to at least make improvements to his company's hiring and development processes that didn't cost a lot. We both knew that underneath Alan's gruff exterior was a truly wonderful and caring human being and a champion triathlon athlete who was trying his best to get his company where he knew it had to be.

The real break-through came on a very warm August day as he and I were sitting on his apartment balcony overlooking East Seventy-Fourth Street and York Avenue. As usual, Alan was telling me all the reasons he couldn't make any major changes while complaining bitterly about his competitors and employees. I was once again trying to explain things he could do to fix the problems. Even though he was writing down everything I was saying, I knew he would go back to the office and get so wound up in the day-to-day operations of his business that he'd forget about the ideas we had discussed.

Determined that this time I was going to get him into action, I threw caution to the wind: "Alan," I said, "all you do is give me hundreds of reasons why you can't do anything. You've been in business for fifty-one years. You know *exactly* what you have to do." Alan paused, thought for a few moments and eventually put his pen down. He then proceeded to outline exactly what he needed to do.

He indeed took action and let several employees go, especially salespeople who kept missing their targets and were otherwise underperforming. To clarify roles and expertise, he reorganized his sales team into two different groups: business developers, who would be out on the road wooing clients and reminding them of his company's quality service, and experts who would answer phones and not only ensure customers got exactly the tires they wanted when they wanted them, but who also could offer other products Alan had recently added to his product line, like batteries, etc. These experts could also recommend alternative products if a customer's request was out of stock and/or upsell customers on better tires as appropriate. New metrics and commission structures accompanied this change.

Alan invested in an e-commerce site and started selling tires through Amazon. Alan had convinced himself he was a lousy manager and he wouldn't believe that his employees were there because of him, and not in spite of him. He finally understood how much his team valued him when he started organizing regular team meetings and made more effort to talk with his employees instead of communicating via email. His mood brightened and he relaxed enough to begin telling jokes again. A year later he had implemented enough improvements to attract a suitor who eventually bought his company, giving Alan enough of a financial cushion to pursue his athletics and other interests, something he had certainly earned the right to do.

Alan's resistance to disruption has nothing to do with age or experience. I've also seen young entrepreneurs who steadfastly refuse to make necessary disruptions to their companies. In the case of some Gen Xers, Yers and Zers, it is because they have developed belief systems about what it means to be a "socially aware" business which, while highly laudable in theory, can result in decisions more harmful to the growth of a company than helpful.

Being a fair, socially minded entrepreneur can mean many things, but in the case of another one of my clients, Ashish, it meant not firing employees who weren't growing with the company. He had also allowed unusual structures to be put in place because of his concern about rocking the boat too much and/or possibly upsetting some of his direct reports.

The most glaring example was having four people in charge of a business line when one was clearly enough.

Ashish is of East Indian heritage, born in the United States and college educated near Washington, DC. He is smart, charming, low-key, and creative. He is also truly concerned for the well-being of his employees and clients. Ashish founded his software and IT consulting company when he was in his late twenties, ten years before he and I met. The company started in the enterprise portal space, collaborating directly with the Oracle WCI (WebCenter Interaction) portal. The company now offers products and services in data security, web experience management, operational intelligence, web center sites, and project management.

When we started working together, Ashish's company had been bumping up against the $10 million revenue mark for a few years but had not been able to break through that barrier. I call this "The $10 Million Hurdle." For some reason, many entrepreneurs who survive the start-up phase of their company without outside investors or substantial adviser networks often find the next obstacle to growth is passing $10 million in revenue (give or take a few million dollars). A lot of what often gets a company to that point—hard work, keeping a few sustainable clients happy while building new relationships, an often-well-defined product and/or service niche, loyal employees, etc.—doesn't seem to be enough to grow the company beyond that point.

What makes this story so interesting is that Ashish was being told by his employees exactly what to change, but because of his fixed way of seeing the world, himself, and his business, Ashish chose to do nothing. (Alan wasn't even giving his employees a chance to share their ideas until he asked me to talk with them.)

The first thing we did was to set up a process to choose one person out of the four leaders of Ashish's largest business line to run the practice. We narrowed the list down to the two best candidates based on a set of leadership criteria. Ashish then asked both of them to present their ideas separately regarding how he or she would run the business. Well, Ashish never made it to that point, because the two contenders got together and decided on their own who the better candidate was. In addition, the gentleman who conceded actually helped the winner write her presentation.

That event was enough to convince Ashish to get back on the playing field and stay one step ahead of the team before they started making all the decisions that he should have been making.

SECTION 23

Getting into Action

Whether you are a new CEO, a long-standing leader of an organization, or the owner of a small, medium-sized, or very large company, many of the capabilities required to plan and execute successful smaller or internal disruptions are the same.

As we saw in part three, you should be able to draw on your experience and instincts as well as take advantage of as many of the sources of data available to you to make good—and often counterintuitive—decisions. Maybe you have already overseen some sort of annual strategic planning exercise and have developed some good skills when it comes to planning, holding people accountable, and following through during execution. If not, then you should find someone with those capabilities to support you to add to your team.

When executing even the smallest disruption, you will quickly discover that the most challenging parts are the inevitable cultural, psychological, and emotional issues you will have to deal with. Dealing effectively with these softer parts of your business will require great emotional intelligence and excellent leadership skills.

But if you have been leading your company for an extended period of time, perhaps the most difficult part will be dealing with yourself. The work you did in part two will come in handy, except now you will be completely exposed and vulnerable in front of a group of people, not just yourself and maybe a few trusted advisors.

Leave your ego at home and be mentally prepared to look bad in front of people who trust and respect you. (And for the record, if you don't return that trust and respect, then you might be in bigger trouble than you think.) If that caring is in place, life will be a lot easier, especially if you start making decisions that appear at first glance to go against many things

123

you have decided in the past or could be painful to your team. Let yourself be vulnerable and your team will follow you, but also communicate the facts and data you used to come to your big-bang conclusions.

True and lasting rebirth usually can only be brought about by disruption. By the time the worst is over, an organization is ready to move on to new and greater challenges. Friends and colleagues may have been let go or left of their own accord. Remaining employees may feel their roles have changed to such a degree that they don't understand what the future holds. It's a strange phenomenon, but those who are left often feel guilty that they survived, believing that those who were let go somehow had their careers and lives destroyed.

But once you tell your company about a key decision you have made, make sure there's a detailed plan with those people who will be accountable to execute it. Never waver or find excuses to deviate from the path, regardless of how difficult or painful some of the activities, such as laying off people, reorganizing, or cutting out old products and services may be.

Sometimes small, internal changes have a far greater impact on a business than bigger and riskier external disruptions. Contact us at **www.JohnFFurth.com** to learn to identify the real issues that are getting in the way of your company's performance. We can also help you plan and implement internal disruptions that put your business back on track quickly and relatively painlessly.

PART SIX

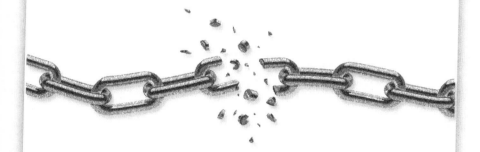

DARE TO IMAGINE A BETTER WORLD

SECTION 24

Say Goodbye to the Past

I met Rob when I connected with him on LinkedIn and asked if he had a few minutes to talk on the phone. As the founder of what looked to me like a pretty innovative company, I wanted to tell him about my Vistage group of business owners and CEOs. If there was a fit with Vistage's value proposition and our styles meshed well, then maybe he'd consider becoming a member.

During our initial phone call, Rob talked animatedly about the business he had started four years earlier. His vision was to increase competitive pricing, liquidity, and transparency, initially in the variable-rate sector of the municipal bond market, while making it more accessible to any size investor, even the smallest. Rob was on a mission to disrupt and transform a niche market with wide-ranging possibilities for doing the same for other asset classes.

That was interesting stuff, I said. Did he have time for an interview for a book I was writing about the best practices of business disruption?

Rob was intrigued enough to agree to an hour meeting at his office on the forty-third floor of the Chrysler building. I guess he thought he might get some free PR to support his efforts at building his company's brand. If nothing else, maybe he'd learn something new. On my side, I was planning to be in the area that day anyway, and there was a good chance I'd get some interesting insights to add to this book.

Unexpectedly for both of us, that first interview turned into a series of probing and thoughtful conversations that covered a lot of territory, from brush stroke techniques in painting to hot new restaurants in New York City to the pricing of fixed-income securities. We quickly discovered that our respective journeys had taken us to many of the same places, intellectually and spiritually.

Passion and a desire to communicate with people on a deeper level makes Rob a compelling storyteller who ropes in the listener quickly. Although there are vestiges of his former big-bank-market-operator persona, as we got deeper into his story, a truer, more authentic, and vulnerable Rob came through, which in turn made his story that much more interesting.

Rob had never felt like his life was only about being a trader/banker. His first love was and still is food and art. Had his grandparents stayed in Italy, he would have most likely pursued the artistic side of his personality more, but the practical needs of paying bills and starting a family in the United States at the end of the twentieth century took priority.

At the age of twenty-two, Rob started his Wall Street career as an assistant to the traders on the fixed-income desk at Smith Barney Harris Upham & Company, not at all certain whether this was going to lead to anything in the long term. That was in 1991.

Within a year and a half, Rob had become a trader at Smith Barney covering a variety of securities classes, including certificates of deposit, commercial paper, auction rate securities (ARS), variable-rate demand bonds, and municipal notes. Over the next decade, he successfully climbed his way up the proverbial corporate ladder. And when, after several changes of ownership, Smith Barney went from a boutique traditional dealer to a major global player as part of Citigroup, Rob became the head of the ARS desk. He and his team covered securities ranging from tax-exempt debt to taxable asset-backed securities (ABS) debt and corporate preferred stock.

His success continued unabated at Citigroup. From 2002 until 2007, he and his team grew the bank's ARS book of business from $22 billion to $72 billion, generating hundreds of millions of dollars in annual revenue for the bank. In 2007 Rob was named the head of all the short-term, tax-exempt syndicate and trading desks as well as the head of the tax-exempt and taxable ARS portfolio.

But in the heady days of July 2007, and at the top of his game, Rob became an unwitting participant in the first tremor of an oncoming earthquake. It was precisely those asset classes that Rob had built his success on, and for which he was a major market maker, that were causing a panic: collateralized debt obligations (CDOs)—an ABS product—and municipal bonds.

From his seat at the trading desks of Citigroup in New York, Rob watched as the markets disintegrated, turning relationships that had existed for years upside-down. When all the shaking stopped, Citigroup was holding billions of dollars of paper—an unusually high amount, even for a major global bank. The resulting intensity and pressure in the months that followed were unlike anything Rob had experienced before or since. He was not only facing the ever-looming threat of regulatory intervention but also a career that could have been easily ruined forever.

Rob was by no means alone. Executives at the rating agencies, senior bankers at other large banks, the most senior management at Citigroup, as well as individual and institutional investors were all part of a very specific ecosystem. They were part of what was to be later seen as the beginning of the worst global financial crisis since 1929.

Deep down, Rob knew he had to do something to disrupt and transform the situation, but first, he had to fix some major short-term problems.

SECTION 25

Rethinking Ecosystems and Processes

James F. Moore originated the concept of business ecosystems about the same time Clayton Christensen developed his first ideas about business disruption. The basic definition comes from Moore's book, *The Death of Competition: Leadership and Strategy in the Age of Business Ecosystems.*

Briefly stated, Moore says that an ecosystem is a community of interacting organizations and individuals that produces goods and services of value to customers. Members of an ecosystem include suppliers, lead producers, competitors, and other stakeholders. In every ecosystem, a leader or a group of leaders are valued by the community because they enable members to move toward shared visions to better decide on their investments and to find mutually supportive roles.[13]

That is, until someone comes along and disrupts the whole thing.

Some disruptions alter an ecosystem when a company—sometimes one that was never even part of the ecosystem to begin with—takes power and influence from an existing leader. But truly big and transformative disruptions can only really occur when an ecosystem is forced to put its end users, who had until then been subsidiary to other, more powerful constituencies, firmly at the center of all activities of the system.

In Rob's story, ten years after the financial meltdown, large banks still dominated most aspects of trading, including the flow of information, by managing liquidity in fixed-income markets. When investors are convinced a market is illiquid, they tend to trade the asset class less frequently, far more cautiously, and then often only through the most

---

[13] Moore, James F. *The Death of Competition: Leadership and Strategy in the Age of Business Ecosystems.* HarperBusiness, 1997.

knowledgeable brokers. And because the banks have so much control, they have the power to determine the interest rates and therefore the value of the paper in circulation.

Unfortunately, it was exactly this one-sided control that caused the problems in 2007. The scarcity of transparency in Rob's markets helped cause illiquidity—an extraordinary situation which an outdated market construct was not prepared to deal with. Simply put, nobody wanted to buy paper that was in some cases losing tremendous value, depending on existing structures.

I find visualizing an industry's ecosystem and then determining which parts are inefficient, too expensive, or simply unnecessary a great way to think through a disruption conceptually, per the example below.

The Ecosystem of the Municipal Bond Market Before 2007*

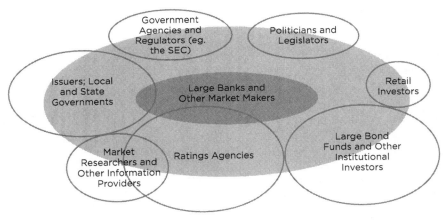

*The size of the bubble approximates the relative level of influence of other players in the marketplace.

The municipal bond market was particularly subject to the will of large institutions. Its ecosystem had changed very little over the past decades. Even ten years after the crisis, most transactions were still handled manually over the phone. Like many markets that have resisted innovation for generations, the powerful few had forced the other players to play the game their way.

Until 2007, all the players in the market—except the investors—profited from the scarcity of data and had no problem changing their analyses to suit the needs of the other important participants. Nobody questioned the quality or depth of their work if the ratings met the standards that the investors set.

Local and state governments, meanwhile, weren't interested in changing a system that gave them access to capital when they needed it. While a few of them may have wondered whether there might be a better way of financing their needs, there was certainly little or no motivation to bite the hand that fed them. Small wonder that regulators let the then-current way of issuing and trading municipal bonds run uninterrupted until the ecosystem ground to a halt in the summer of 2007, which then spread to other financial ecosystems. And despite the rash of regulations that followed in the wake of the financial crisis, not much has really changed in the last ten years.

Having spent eighteen years of his life learning every aspect of the fixed-income business, especially in variable-rate municipal bonds, Rob felt he was one of the only people who had the knowledge and expertise necessary to take on the challenge of changing the situation.

As clear as his journey may seem in hindsight, it wasn't so well-defined to Rob in the months after he left Citigroup. He had always invested in restaurants and considered opening one or two himself while pursuing his art and/or other entrepreneurial ventures full-time. But he kept getting pulled back into his old world and found himself proof-testing his ideas about a disruptive, fixed-income trading business with former colleagues, experts, friends, and other entrepreneurs.

The market for municipal bonds in the United States is not very large compared to other financial security markets—about $3.7 trillion of muni bonds paper is outstanding, compared to about $37 trillion for the entire bond market. Total issuance of new bonds in 2015 was about $347 billion. Rob felt there would be less competition from other potentially disruptive entrepreneurs in a narrowly specific sector with few experts left who have the detail-oriented, specialist knowledge required to be successful. Even if he captured just a fraction of the variable-rate market, he'd be doing well.

After much planning, Rob assembled the perfect team and formed an aggressive business model he felt was worth the risk.

Rob's company developed an electronic Dutch auction platform that issues and trades variable-rate securities accessible to any investor. The activity on this platform, in turn, generates large amounts of reliable and rich data which gives both municipalities and investors a depth of knowledge and a level of comfort often lacking in their dealings with the big banks.

While the road has been very difficult, Rob's bet is starting to pay off. He and his team have handled several significant transactions for several states, and they add multiple private investors and investor groups to the platform daily. No one, however, including Rob, knows if their activities are going to be successful enough to be truly transformative.

You don't always have to be an expert in an industry to disrupt it. In fact, sometimes coming from the outside makes it easier to look at a potentially better solution with an unencumbered and more innovative perspective.

My friend Dov is that kind of disruptive entrepreneur. His expertise is of a more functional nature—he is a former systems and data scientist with the Israeli military and a seasoned entrepreneur, having built and sold multiple companies. Dov is soft-spoken and more prone to let facts speak for themselves rather than wind himself up into a sales and marketing frenzy. This also has a lot to do with the industry he is currently working in, healthcare, which tends to be more understated than the financial industry.

Once Dov decided to focus his entrepreneurial efforts on the US healthcare system, he discovered the extent to which the push to lower the costs of health care was forcing many patients to leave the hospital before they should. Left on their own, these patients experienced dangerous relapses that could require returning to the hospital, ultimately adding, not subtracting, costs. Because the Affordable Care Act defined financial incentives for hospitals to prevent patient readmissions within a month, there was an opportunity for others outside the current system to deliver greater postoperative patient management.

Being the excellent systems engineer he is, Dov mapped out the "typical" rehabilitation process that most patients in the United States deal with. Initially, he thought by pinpointing every possible breakdown throughout the process that could result in potentially life-threatening situations he'd have a workable solution. But Dov soon discovered everyone was making decisions except the person most affected by those decisions—the patient. He simply couldn't understand why patients and their care teams weren't fully empowered.

That's when he knew he had found an opportunity. But unlike Rob, Dov was less interested in rattling the cages of an entire ecosystem than he was in improving a patient's cycle of care—or process—from the start of a hospital stay to final recovery.

He began building a digital platform, and the first module came from a related but far less regulated industry—fitness training. He took the basic fitness plan that tens of thousands of trainers use to plan day-by-day exercises for their clients to achieve their goals without a lot of supervision. By automating it and putting it on the web, Dov provided a tool for patients and their caregivers to plan, track, and monitor rehabilitation regimes.

The secret sauce, however, is how Dov is using his expertise in systems integration and data science within the complex health care ecosystem. Because his company is small and aggressive, it can quickly adapt and make changes to its approach when necessary. Unlike large, siloed IT companies such as IBM, Dov can design and integrate many other important parts of the care process, including remote patient monitoring, care management, patient engagement, statistical analysis, and social engagement into this platform faster and at far lower cost, while also having the flexibility to integrate with other health care systems used by his platform customers.

His fully automated and highly integrated care management system gives the patient more power to determine the pace and location of his or her recovery—ideally at home—as long as he or she follows the steps that have been entered into her program by her doctor and/or physical therapist. It minimizes the need for extended hospital stays and cumbersome visits to a doctor, hospital, and/or health care professional while being certain a patient is constantly monitored for progress remotely.

Although they are coming at their respective solutions from different vantage points, Rob and Dov are similar in recognizing the immense value of the data they can collect in more transparent and automated systems. Dov and his engineers can provide important data and analytics not usually available to patients to help them adhere to their regimens, thereby better guaranteeing improvements to their health.

Dov and Rob are also united in their desire to democratize outmoded approaches that have been traditionally dominated by large, entrenched players who cede little or no power to the consumer, end-user, or patient. Rob can hardly wait for the day when Citigroup bankers wake up to the immense change taking place right in front of their eyes and then unsuccessfully scramble to put together the kind of automated marketplace he has already introduced.

Likewise, Dov feels safe in the knowledge that while other bigger and better-known companies may have pieces for a managed care platform, they will never be able to pull together the kind of integrated solution offered by his company.

SECTION 26

What Stays the Same

Perhaps the most disruptive statement about disruption came from the master himself, Jeff Bezos. Being ready for the future isn't about seeing the big changes in advance, Bezos opined in 2015; successful disruptions are more about understanding what things will *stay the same* than going out and simply disrupting everything under the sun. This understanding has resonated with thousands of leaders and has become one of the most important learnings for potential disruptors.

But what exactly stays the same?

At the most basic level, every successful business—disruptive or otherwise, B2B or B2C—needs to address at least one of the following core truths. In its pursuit of being "the most consumer-centric company in the world," Amazon manages to address all three of them, all the time:

- Provide goods, services and experiences that were previously only available to the most privileged members of society to a much larger percentage of the population more easily and affordably.

- Give customers what they want, when they want it, and how they want it.

- Eliminate or reduce everyday annoyances like wasted time, boredom, complexity, or unhappiness as well as life-threatening situations like poverty and disease.

In many ways, Rob's and Dov's companies respect these basic principles and use them as the foundation for their disruptive businesses, whether it was a conscious decision or not. They go even further in recognizing that there are limits to just how much of the existing ecosystems or processes can be radically changed and transformed at this stage in their companies' journeys.

For one, they currently don't have millions of dollars to burn through, and neither of them is thinking of an IPO in the foreseeable future. Given their extensive business experience, they each also understand just how much risk they're willing to take to achieve their goals.

For another, as large as their dreams are, neither Rob nor Dov have the ambitions to be the next Jeff Bezos, Bill Gates, or Elon Musk.

In fact, a closer look at Rob's and Dov's businesses shows that really they are also making only one or two strategic and significant disruptions to existing systems. They both use existing technologies. While their outputs are a richer and better experience for the end users, they both work with the same basic constituents that are already in place in their respective ecosystems. Although they would like to lessen the power of larger players, they also realize that at some point, they will probably have to play nice with them.

Much the same can be said for Lyft and Uber, LinkedIn, and many other highly successful companies, with the exception that they really aren't interested in playing nice with any of their competitors.

The moral of Sean's story in section nine is that he disrupted too much in an effort to keep up with the market, instead of picking one or two things to focus on. He's now learned that lesson and is being far more careful—and successful.

This rule of "more stays the same than changes in disruption" applies to every successful business disruption. While many would-be disruptive leaders might get the above value proposition right, if they disrupt too much at the same time or disregard important business principals, they run the risk of destroying everything they worked to build.

SECTION 27

Timing and Technology

The question of whether technologies—new and existing—or strategically thought-through business models are the more important ingredient for great disruptive businesses has been debated for decades. The one side firmly believes that without advances in technology, even the best disruptive businesses never get past the idea phase. The other side argues that technology doesn't cause disruptions—it's business people's ideas that have the power to disrupt and transform people's lives.

The fact is both are equally important. Most big and audacious disruptions start with someone identifying a problem, want or need for which there is no widely available solution. Sometimes the right technology that could potentially provide a platform for a disruptive business hasn't been developed yet but sometimes no one has figured out how to make money by inventing a solution to a particular issue.

Uber and Lyft, for example, developed an easy-to-use mobile solution to a perennial urban problem—individuals having to stand at curbside, often in terrible weather conditions, trying to hail a taxi. Their solution also gives people living in rural areas who are not able to drive a car themselves have access to cheaper and more convenient individual transportation.

Of course, car services have existed as long as taxicabs, but they often require prebooking, long telephone conversations, and considerable expense. Taxis and limousine services are also subject to complicated and daunting regulations that arose out of safety concerns with licensing models that could be cost-prohibitive for most potential drivers.

As simple as the concept is, however, Uber's, Lyft's and other such companies' business models was only possible when the right mobile technology had been developed.

The digital revolution, which has already had one of the most transformative impacts in the recorded history of the world, started in earnest at the beginning of the 1990s. Until then, the prevailing thinking was that users were slow in adopting disruptive technologies. And to a certain degree this was true, as so much technology—especially for businesses—involved significant investment in equipment and infrastructure. Often, new technology was often difficult to learn to use or highly counterintuitive which required many hours of training.

In contrast, the newest digital and mobile technologies are inexpensive, simple to install and use. Most importantly, they have automatically leveled the playing field for entrepreneurs around the world.

When it comes to the subject of timing and technology there are two popular myths I'd like to debunk. The biggest myth of all is the belief that "unicorns" exist in business—that is, companies whose unique solutions to big problems provide them with high barriers to entry that protect them from potentially disruptive competitors.

On the contrary, I would say that if you can't find anyone else trying to compete in the space you have defined, the opportunity is most likely not that attractive, at least not at that particular time. The greater the opportunity, the faster players will jump on it.

Patents certainly help to sustain some sort of competitive advantage, but aggressive entrepreneurs have proven adept at developing alternative technologies that often offer similar solutions. Their lawyers can circumvent existing patents and/or successfully apply for new ones. In the software industry, a slight change in a string of code can be enough justification for a new patent. In other industries, a modification to a process or a slight variation in outcome can be sometimes enough to justify awarding the inventor a new patent. The consumer rarely knows the difference.

The other myth that has blinded many otherwise intelligent people to the realities of life and business is an unfounded belief in what we often call the "first mover advantage." I can't think of any instance when a business had a significant and sustainable advantage because they were the first one out the door. In fact, it's often the first movers who get disrupted the fastest. Most first movers get trampled in the dust simply because someone else has more money, a better plan, or a more developed organization. Sometimes first movers are up against savvier entrepreneurs, or they simply aren't at the right place at the right time.

About fifteen years ago I worked at a start-up with a team of senior executives and technology experts we firmly believed had a first mover advantage that would mow everything down in its path forward until we discovered quite the opposite was true.

I took a year off in 2001/2002 before joining Sony and spent the time working with a few small companies. One of them had purchased the rights to technology developed by the military to harvest intelligence "buried" in thousands of documents. It was essentially an early version of e-discovery software that would take off several years later.

The CEO of the company wanted to repurpose the software as a business development tool for professional service companies. Hundreds of thousands of documents comprising both structured and unstructured data found on a company's servers and/or employees' hard drives could be fed into the tool. These documents would be scoured by powerful search engines which in turn could find hidden connections between individuals that were not otherwise evident without a lot of manual processing. A salesperson or business developer could then map out a path of connections to eventually get in front of an important target client.

We were clearly a few years ahead of our time, and the software had a lot of bugs. In addition, poor economic conditions at the time made it almost impossible to get the funding necessary to fix the problems and develop the software to the point at which it could process huge amounts of data. Within a year, the money that the founders had invested disappeared, and I went to work for the CEO of Sony in Japan.

About five years later I was invited to "link in" with a former employee of mine and quickly realized that our basic idea had been further developed and refined. Using a much friendlier user interface and a process that didn't rely on countless proprietary documents, but instead on building an open community of users, a company named LinkedIn used similar connection-mining technology to become the leader in online B2B business development and recruitment.

And let's not forget that Facebook had its forerunners as well—most notably MySpace, which in subsequent years has become not much more than a footnote in the annals of online social networking services.

SECTION 28

Insights, Inspiration, and Ideas

No idea has ever popped out of someone's head without a lot of work. Even a genius like Edison didn't wake up one day with a fully formed idea for the light bulb. So be prepared for a lot of false starts, and don't forget—talk to as many people as possible to refine your thinking, learn something new, or to simply get a reality check.

If all else fails and your brain just isn't kicking in properly, look at some of the suggestions in this book and/or think about major changes in other industries that have made a significant improvement in your quality of life. It's important that you really understand the ins and outs of the individual, discrete elements that came together to make that happen.

But that also means you need to understand if there are other companies out there tackling the same issue, what their solutions are and how your company is going to stay competitive over the long haul to stay ahead of the pack. Traditionally, most companies achieved long-term competitive advantage by building high barriers to entry, usually in the form of large investments or multiple patents that protected their products, processes, or some other proprietary aspect of their business. They could also use mildly disruptive activities such as making a high-quality or lower-cost product or service and delivering it better or faster to drive competitors out of the market.

In today's world, almost any aspect of a business model—not just product attributes or the efficiency of the supply chain—can prove to be a competitive advantage, even if it's only for a short period of time. While patents still offer a certain amount of protection, traditional high investments in fixed assets are often unnecessary when starting a successful business. Everything, from the quality of the talent you hire and the velocity at which you hire them to the location of your business to the investors you bring on board, the branding and positioning of your company's products or services to optimized processes and systems, can turn out to be a distinctive advantage against your competitors.

Finally, there is the simple question of practicality. Sometimes the hurdles that a new and theoretically better solution faces are so numerous and/or monumental as to make it unwise to invest a lot of time, money, and effort in implementing a solution until those issues have been thought through.

I have developed a process I use with clients to help them turn disruptive ideas into actual products and services. Each step has a set of criteria that have to be met before an idea can move to the next phase. You can find a worksheet that is easy to use and provides greater detail at **www.JohnFFurth.com/worksheets**.

STEP 1: Generate a List of Ideas – Disruptive innovations always start with a tangible problem or a desire/need that hasn't yet found an inexpensive and easily replicated solution. Leaders and teams who aspire to develop and market disruptive products and services should compile and update a list of ideas they have thought of themselves or have heard about at conferences, when reading books, talking to clients, etc.

STEP 2: Research Solutions Already on The Market – Just because it might appear there is no product or service to fulfill a strong need or desire doesn't means it doesn't already exist. It's possible, for example, that the perfect product is on the market but nobody has recognized it as an answer to that particular issue. However, if viable solutions do exist, then your team needs to evaluate whether those products are as effective, efficient, and/or well-priced as potential alternatives could be.

You can then decide if it's worth the effort to develop a better and more disruptive product or service. If it doesn't make sense, I suggest putting that idea on hold and turning your attention to another opportunity.

STEP 3: Turn Your Idea into Disruptive Products and Services
– At this point your team should start evaluating how to find the best combination of technologies and business models that will turn an interesting idea into a very real, usable product or service. Once you are far enough along, you will need to understand if this new product fulfills at least one of the three key value propositions discussed in section five of this book. As the last action in this step, take the definition of disruption I use in section one (which can also be found in the process document on my website) to understand if you have a truly disruptive product or just an incrementally innovative one.

STEP 4: Test Viability – The first activity in this step is to determine whether the addressable market for your product is large enough so you can attract the talent and funding necessary to ensure success. This is also the time you and your team need to ensure there are a few barriers to entry— such as patents, expensive infrastructure, use of strategic partnerships, etc. —in place so you won't in turn be disrupted. Last but not least, have your team assess whether there are any regulatory, cultural, or legal hurdles that if confronted head on could spell disaster for your business.

Only until a product or service has made it through all four steps can your team move onto planning the launch of the new product or service.

Go to **www.JohnFFurth.com/worksheets** to download the easy-to-use process document described above.

PART SEVEN

PUTTING THE FINAL PIECES IN PLACE

SECTION 29

The Disruptive Organization

I t may sound simplistic but all the best disruptive ideas and visions in the world mean nothing if there is no organization to implement them or if the organization is incapable of meeting the demands of a disruptive strategy.

Every successful company—disruptive or otherwise—lives and dies by the ability of its employees to consistently plan and execute on a daily basis as well as over much longer increments of time. As we saw in part three annual and longer-term planning is best done using an annual company-wide strategic planning exercise.

Strategic planning, accountability, and performance tracking as well as decision-making are a few of the processes that should be in place by the time a company begins operations. Work flow processes follow close behind, especially as they relate to receiving and making payments (e.g., AR and AP), product development, sales and marketing, etc.

While disruptive organizations can look and feel to an outsider much like other companies, they have their own particular traits. Many disruptive companies are set from the very beginning on a high growth trajectory. For this they need the requisite funding to make the right investments, something we'll discuss in section thirty-one. And like any well-functioning business, it's imperative for them as well to maintain a healthy cash flow so they can pay employees, suppliers, and cover expenses, even when, as was the case for many years at Amazon, every penny is being reinvested in the business.

High growth disruptive companies also need the agility to not only manage the day-to-day business but also quickly define and implement other key processes for example for HR (e.g., recruitment, hiring, development, retention, and separation), choosing and managing suppliers and partners as well as more complex product manufacturing systems and/or services/technology development, etc. while also updating processes that are no longer able to support an organization growing by leaps and bounds.

In part one I wrote about how important it is for a company's CEO to provide a compelling mission as a guidepost for planning as well as high-level and daily decision-making. This is especially true for disruptive organizations where it's easy for employees to lose site of goals in the midst of the inevitable chaos. Jeff Bezos's mission statement for Amazon—"to be Earth's most customer-centric company"—gives him and his leadership team a tool to constantly remind their far-flung organization of what they're all working towards.

And yet, some disruptive business leaders disregard basic organizational principals or ignore the signs that the organization is not growing with the business.

You'll read in the next section how one famous CEO—Travis Kalanick of Uber—almost destroyed his company by not addressing pressing organization issues such as:

- Building a culture of core values that are inspiring, respectful, and constructive.

- Having the right people doing the rights things at the right time.

- Understanding the regulatory, legal, and ethical limits of the society you are operating in and pick your battles carefully.

At the end of the day, all organizations are growing, changing, and mutating organisms made up of human beings with all their qualities and all their faults. Great disruptive leaders understand that often the difference between great success and abject failure is the degree to which they can keep and develop the best talent the world has to offer, which in itself can be a highly disruptive idea for many business people.

SECTION 30

Do You Have a Team of Champions or a Team of Chumps?

isruptive leaders may surround themselves with the skill sets and experiences they believe they need to overcome obstacles and create great advances for their business and the world. They are happiest, however, when they are working with like-minded souls who at heart live and breathe the same principles they do. It's not uncommon for such leaders to assemble a group of executives they know and trust that stays with them for decades.

Bezos learned early on how to put together high-performing teams. He also learned the importance of using some simple but very powerful tools to develop and keep this team focused on the right things, especially as the organization grew and he no longer managed many of the people he had hired. We refer to these tools as "core values" or "leadership principles."

Even a cursory look at Amazon's leadership principles shows the extent to which Bezos's values and beliefs have been codified, disseminated, and internalized by Amazon's leadership team. While such traits as customer obsession, thinking big, and delivering results may sound pretty generic for millions of companies, there are a few eye-openers on the list, such as frugality, understanding how to be right as much as possible, and diving deeply that are unique to Bezos and Amazon.

These leadership principles continue to be practiced, reinforced, and lived every day around the world by everyone who works at Amazon.

I talked earlier about the impetus behind Rob's decision to start a company. Once Rob had a plan to disrupt the staid world of fixed-income sales and trading, he built the right team to implement his vision. Rob put together a list of core values he then used to make key hiring decisions. Many people approached him to join his team, but not everyone made the cut. Rob wanted a team made up of people who were:

- Broad thinkers
- Creative
- Well-rounded, with many interests outside of work
- Lifelong learners
- Hard-working
- Mentally flexible
- Unconventional
- Committed to getting things done

On the other end of the spectrum is another highly disruptive company: Uber. In mid-2017, the company found itself at the center of a regulatory, press, and societal storm that posed serious threats to its existence.

Travis Kalanick, Uber's cofounder and the company's CEO until mid-June 2017, broke so many rules about basic organizational structure and culture as to call into question his ability to lead the company. Eight years after it was founded, the company was still operating without a CEO, COO, CFO, CMO, or president. A cult of personality and ego which celebrated a highly aggressive culture had taken hold.

On June 6, 2017, news broke that twenty employees had been fired over harassment, discrimination, and inappropriate behavior several days earlier. This was the first public sign that Uber was trying to contain the fallout from a series of toxic revolutions.

A week later, Travis Kalanick was fired, although he still retained a seat on Uber's board. His success and ego had not only blinded him to the need to build a culture of accountability and ethics, but also the need to adhere to local and state employment laws.

A report on Uber's problems with sexism tied most of the problems to Uber's deeply embedded culture of "stepping on toes" and "always be hustlin." While these behaviors might work for a small start-up, they can be highly destructive for a nearly 12,000-person company.

Uber's new CEO since August 2017, Dara Khosrowshahi, faces a long list of challenges he had rarely, if ever, faced as CEO of Expedia. Although he is rightly focused on creating a new culture and values system for Uber, he also has to contend with an array of legacy issues and liabilities, including multiple lawsuits. One lawsuit that is drawing public attention involves Waymo, a smaller competitor, which is suing Uber for stealing trade secrets. After a federal judge determined in November 2017 that Uber had been withholding important evidence in the trial, he declared he could no longer trust Uber's lawyers.

Meanwhile, customers are choosing to ride with drivers of companies such as Lyft, which might have grown more slowly but also have taken the time to build constructive and supportive corporate cultures. These rivals have been raising billions abroad and are banding together. In addition, important cities such as London and Montreal have threatened to either cancel or not renew Uber's licenses.

Several large Uber investors recently marked down their investments in the wake of the company losing $2.8 billion in 2016, as Kalanick drove aggressive growth.

But the thing Khosrowshahi might have to be most concerned about is that, with Kalanick on the board, he might just have a Steve Jobs-type disruption on his hands if Kalanick makes a play to return to his old job of CEO.

SECTION 31

Other People's Money

In our advanced capitalist system—even with cheaper and readily available technology—nothing significant happens without money. And when I say money, I mean huge amounts of it.

Ambitious entrepreneurs at some point or other generally have to find investors or some sort of outside funding to take their companies to the next level. While these days everyone with a disruptive idea seems to be preparing for a Series A round of financing, the truth is that often executives of a new company will waste so much time running after venture capital (VC) and private equity (PE) firms to raise money, they lose focus and often have to close the business when nothing comes of the effort.

But enough entrepreneurs have secured vast amounts of funding that helped them realize their visions, it's worth taking a closer look at what Series A funding entails while considering other options.

The table below summarizes the pre-IPO funding of three of the most well-known disruptive companies. The fourth is smaller, but one of the few run by a woman: Care.com. Many other sources of short-term and long-term financing are available for more established, mature companies. But that is a topic for another day and another book.

Funding by VC and PE companies has become important for entrepreneurs exactly because it can take quite a bit of capital to move from being a start-up with high potential to a significant game-changing multinational company. And only one of the CEOs listed below invested more than $1 million in the company. The bulk of initial funding came from PE firms.

Elon Musk—one of the founders of PayPal and the current CEO of Tesla—is not the founder of Tesla, but started out as an investor and board member, eventually becoming CEO in 2008. He was the largest single investor before Tesla went public and contributed a total of $70 million as lead investor in four rounds.

Company	Examples of Pre-IPO Investors	Period of Fundraising	Funds Raised	Date of IPO	Market Value at IPO	Annualized Revenue/ EBITDA at Time of IPO
Amazon	Bezos and family, Tom Alberg, Kleiner Perkins Caufield Byers	1994-1996	$9.5	May 15, 1997	$483	$147.8/($31)
Tesla	Elon Musk, Daimler-Benz	2004-2007	$105	June 29, 2010	$1,700	$116.7/($146.8)
LinkedIn	Reid Hoffman, friends and family, Sequoia Capital	2003-2010	$85	May 19, 2011	$4,500	$522.2/$98.7
Care.com	Matrix Partners, Reid Hoffman, Trinity Ventures, New Enterprise Associates, USAA, IVP	2006-2012	$111	Jan. 14, 2014	$445	$59/($24.7)

All dollar amounts are in millions.

There are many reasons why raising money from well-known financiers in exchange for equity—or convertible notes—can be a smart move, despite all the difficulties in getting deals done:

- A first round of funding from well-known investors sends a signal that the successful company survived one of the greatest ordeals in business—convincing other people to give them money. It doesn't necessarily mean these companies will ultimately survive and grow, but at least they have demonstrated they can pass an important hurdle. With any luck, they'll pass further tests in the future.

- Smart entrepreneurs make sure initial lead investors are well-known within the ecosystems and communities in which the company intends to play. Such investors bring not only capital but relationships, experience, knowledge, and insights that the leadership of the funded entity might need going forward. These marquee names help attract additional investors and propel the company toward a successful IPO.

- Rounds of early-stage funding are also key moments when a company's value to an investor is professionally assessed, thereby answering one of the most important but difficult questions: If this company is going to make an impact, just how large and valuable will that impact be?

But most importantly, having a significant amount of money at its disposal—and a commensurate high valuation—is sometimes the only advantage an emerging company has in an increasingly competitive world. The more capital a start-up has to work with, the more it can experiment, fail, and experiment again until it gets it right.

Going through a Series A, B, or C funding round is grueling, demoralizing, exhausting, and all-consuming. It's a roller-coaster ride with more downs than ups. If the timing is off because the sector the company is operating in isn't favored at the time, or if there are broader economic forces in play, even the best CEO or entrepreneur may not make any headway despite excellent efforts.

I have a client with a good reputation who loves to build and/or turn around technology companies. But having been through the wringer of fundraising one too many times, his decision when taking on a new CEO role often hinges on the degree to which he is expected to go out and raise capital to get a company back in shape. For the most part, he rightfully turns down a lot of offers if he feels fundraising efforts would distract him from operating the business and play havoc with his family life.

And he's not the only one. I've seen plenty of experienced and outwardly successful CEOs with good track records literally beaten down by this process.

Even the illustrious names in the table above didn't find the process easy. Based on their success and their current stature, many people assume these famous business leaders could have raised money in the blink of an eye. The reality is that the process of raising funds for their first companies required as much hard work and dealing with skepticism and rejection as any other aspiring entrepreneur.

The story of Reid Hoffman's experience with LinkedIn's Series A as told in 2011 by one of his first key executives, Lee Hower, highlights the key areas every VC will drill down on: the company's basic concept, plausibility of its five-year plan, and the perceived ability of the CEO and his management team to execute that plan.[14]

When Reid Hoffman started LinkedIn out of his Mountain View apartment at the end of 2002, Silicon Valley was still emerging from the tech bubble and massive downturn of late 2000-2002. The market size for online advertising, e-commerce and web premium services was one-tenth of the size it was in 2017.

Online social networking was a concept still being evangelized. Facebook didn't exist, even as a walled-garden college social network (Mark Zuckerberg was in his first year at Harvard). There were no social platforms to build on. It would be nearly two years before the concept of "Web 2.0" was popularized by Tim O'Reilly.

Reid Hoffman might have been a very successful PayPal executive, but this was his first time as a CEO. Although he already was an investor in Friendster and one or two other companies, this was long before Hoffman was a legendary angel with investments in Facebook, Zynga, etc.

Hoffman assembled the founding team, drawing largely from his prior start-ups, along with a few other folks he'd known for a long time. He provided initial seed funding to launch the LinkedIn website publicly on May 5, 2003, and a month or two later, Hoffman and his team began talking to VCs for the Series A round. LinkedIn's product had been live for a short couple of months and only had about twenty or thirty thousand registered users. Company leadership didn't expect it would start generating revenue for more than a year.

[14] Shontell, Alyson. "LinkedIn's Lee Hower Describes The Brutal Series A Fundraising Process." May 26, 2011. http://www.businessinsider.com/linkedins-lee-hower-what-it-was-like-raising-the-series-a-round-in-2003-2011-5.

The reactions from most of the firms they talked to were decidedly mixed. The partners at some VC companies couldn't unite behind what some thought was an industry (e.g., the B2C internet) they believed was just a massive waste of time and money. Others got caught up in technical debates about LinkedIn's five-year forecast or Reid's abilities as a first-time CEO. But a couple of firms quickly grasped the opportunity and liked the team and concept.

At the end of the process, Hoffman and his team received term sheets from two firms. The terms and valuation for both offers were comparable, and Hoffman's team felt both firms would have made good partners. They ultimately chose Sequoia Capital's term sheet. It was a $4.7 million round which closed in November 2003, and the pre-money valuation was between $10 million and $15 million.

Ultimately, Hoffman and his team learned that start-up fundraising isn't about convincing skeptics, but more about finding true believers.

This brings us, then, to the last point about why bringing on experienced and well-known financial investors is so important. Their singular focus on financial returns imposes accountability and discipline on the leaders of companies they support. Reid Hoffman's success as a CEO was in part propelled by the ever-present need to produce returns through excellence in execution and leadership. Not only did he quickly grow LinkedIn to $500 million in revenue, but he is also the only CEO on the list above whose company was profitable at the time of its IPO.

But private equity and venture capital funding are not the only options available to entrepreneurs looking to build disruptive businesses who need large amounts of funding to grow. As Rob's story below highlights, a strategic partner who takes a significant stake to propel the growth of a company while providing additional benefits is often preferable.

After he left Citigroup and before he started his company, Rob successfully reassembled former colleagues, from the person who had hired him on Wall Street in 1991 to his former global head, all to start a municipal trading and research effort for a boutique LLC that had been specializing primarily in taxable, fixed-income trading and research.

Rob quickly built a good working relationship with the principals of the LLC and even started a municipal research LLC as his first project, partnering with the LLC. As soon as he had committed to a plan for his then-current business, he approached them for seed funding. They came to an agreement, and Rob's fledgling business became one of the company's divisions.

The LLC was the ideal partner for Rob and his team during the start-up phase of his business. In addition to capital, they also provided basic operational support as well as a much-needed broker dealer license. But after two years, it initially became clear to everyone involved that Rob would need more money to take his company to the next level.

Rob started knocking on the doors of the PE and VC communities, including those on the West Coast. To his dismay, he discovered that the very thing that he was trying to disrupt with his business—an entrenched ecosystem that relegated outsiders to the fringes—was also true of the West Coast investor community. And in some ways, it was an even more closed community than the big bank community he had left. If you don't have very strong ties to Silicon Valley, Rob found, or a track record that is easily recognizable, the effort bears almost no fruit.

Of course, there are also many venture capital and private equity firms based in New York City. But their knowledge of technology and the details of something as specific as his small sector of global capital markets was not sufficiently deep enough to grasp what he was trying to accomplish for the market sector and the annuity model for any future investor to enjoy. And while West Coast financiers had a better understanding of the nuts and bolts of technology, as well as its power to disrupt and transform entire industries and generate incredible returns, their interest in the financial technology sector was limited.

Likewise, Rob's few discussions with mergers and acquisitions shops yielded almost nothing concrete in terms of an investor.

Rob had always looked to Michael Bloomberg as a source of inspiration. As a young entrepreneur, Bloomberg had spent many years going door-to-door hawking his technology. It wasn't until he formed a strategic partnership with Merrill Lynch that he had found the global reach, business sophistication, and back-office systems he needed to give his company the kind of boost he was looking for. At some point, Rob realized that was the route he was meant to take.

Given everything Rob had been through up until early 2017, you'd think approaching the very entities he was in fact trying to disrupt (i.e., large global banks) for some sort of partnership would be a fool's errand. But Rob went there anyway. It was a grueling process that required hundreds of meetings, an equal number of plane trips, and lots of patience. But eventually he found an ideal candidate—a global bank with a solid foundation, but a low presence in Rob's specific sector of the capital markets.

The executives he met there were also looking to leapfrog traditional players and build a better future of capital markets that were more transparent and democratic. They bought into Rob's vision quickly because it was congruent with their vision for other capital market sectors. They also liked the annuity-based revenue stream which the investment and back-end support they provided to Rob's company would pay.

They also found that Rob and his team could make a real impact to other parts of their business, and the concept of a symbiotic relationship became evermore apparent. Despite having now attracted fresh interest from two other major Wall Street firms, Rob's focus and vision have kept him fully engaged with the original partner after so many other possible options that started to present themselves to him once they went live and started building a real buzz in the market.

This new relationship will provide Rob and his team with that extra competitive advantage that a PE or VC company only interested in financial returns could never have provided him. He likes to say that instead of just landing on the moon—something that had already been done a generation earlier—his team now has the vehicle that will take them to Mars, a better fit and goal with the world's aspirations in the new millennium.

No discussion about the bravest and newest world of funding can fail to mention the recent phenomenon of ICOs (Initial Coin Offerings).

My experience with ICOs is limited to what I learned from a business owner who provides IT enterprise solutions to law firms and with whom I was discussing the possibility of joining my Vistage group. Within a two-day period and with the help of his son, a former Morgan Stanley banker, he raised $20 million—an amount greater than his revenue at the time—to upgrade his services and expand his client base. I talked to him shortly after his ICO and he sounded even more amazed than I was ... and I hadn't even heard of ICOs until that moment.

Purchasing coins (better known as cryptocurrencies) in an ICO is essentially like buying shares in a traditional IPO: coins give investors a stake in the issuing company. Sometimes the coins can also be used to purchase the services or products of the issuer as a kind of futures contract or loyalty points program.

However, at the time I was writing this book, cryptocurrencies were only traded on exchanges which weren't very liquid or transparent, often experiencing wild fluctuations in value. There was little need for a "trusted" middleman to run an ICO, and the Securities and Exchange Commission (SEC) was struggling to understand how to regulate them. ICOs were therefore very risky, with only a small number of investors willing to take the plunge.

Once the SEC decides on the proper regulatory framework, and there is more data and transparency available, ICOs will attract larger numbers of investors. I have no doubt they will become one of many avenues for small companies to raise large amounts of capital.

SECTION 32

Selling Disruption

The four Ps of traditional marketing—product, pricing, placement and positioning—hold true for disruption as well. (Remember—in disruption, more stays the same than changes.) Unfortunately, the potential for confusion among end users and other important constituencies is so high when marketing and selling products and services that break traditional paradigms that a misguided campaign can kill a disruption even before it even gets off the ground. That's why a simple and emotional narrative is critical to the success of any disruptive business—B2B, B2C, or otherwise.

A disruptive company's narrative should ideally start with the leader, especially if he or she is particularly charismatic. Disruptors are best framed as revolutionaries, and in parallel, their targets become akin to the "establishment." Steve Jobs is a great example of a high-profile disruptor who was positioned as an outsider/tough-guy intellectual laying waste to the incumbent consumer electronics giants with whom Jobs did battle until he and Apple became bigger and wealthier than they had been.

Earlier I used a few quotes found in the media that tried to describe the personalities of leading disruptors in order to offer a sense of how disparate and unusual their behaviors could be. But these snippets also provided some examples of how the media can further the cause of a disruptive organization with compelling and colorful characterizations of a company's CEO.

- "Jeff Bezos may be a visionary, but when it comes to his business, it seems he also has a bit of a murderous streak. He won't let competitors beat him, even if it means killing his core business." *Jill Krasny, technology writer*

- "Personality tests given to key execs (have) repeatedly shown (Michael) Dell to be an off-the-charts introvert. At its heart is Dell's belief that the status quo is never good enough, even if it means painful changes for the man with his name on the door. When success is achieved, it's greeted with five seconds of praise followed by five hours of postmortem on what could have been done better." *Andrew Park, technology writer*

- "Reed Hastings has a restless, slightly paranoid attitude, combined with a Steve Jobs-like perfectionist streak" *John Doerr, partner at Kleiner Perkins Caufield Byers*

Because customers or end-users are at the center of any meaningful disruption, it is equally important, if not more so, to tell the story of a disruption from their point of view and in language they can relate to. The secret is to capture the fantasy of a customer's future needs while showing that the old paradigm was not serving the consumer—an old way of thinking (not just the service itself) is dead.

Here again, Steve Jobs and his marketing team hit the ball out of the park. Using a short and incredibly powerful marketing slogan, Apple not only caught the public's attention but also captured the essence of what it meant to be a highly disruptive company: "Think Different."

Your product isn't just a product: It solves a problem or pain point for your customers. Sometimes disruptive companies are so forward-thinking, they solve challenges the consumer hasn't even considered—for example, who thought there was another solution to a yellow cab?—so you must identify an even more intrinsic opportunity.

By the same token, anything *too* forward-thinking that doesn't have a compelling narrative will crash and burn, while a trendy-yet-innovative solution with a good story may succeed in the wake of an incumbent's failure.

Ideally narratives should follow the recipe for a good Hollywood plot-twister: start with a situation (e.g., a company) that is going well until it is threatened by an outside force; in rides the hero who not only saves the company but pushes it on to glory, wealth, and a long, sustainable future.

Netflix fit this formula perfectly. Not only did the company have a pretty flamboyant and media-savvy CEO and cofounder, Reed Hastings, but the story about the near-crash-and-burn of the company was exciting, inspiring and, most importantly, easy to understand. Here is my version:

1. **Situation:** Company puts brick-and-mortar movie rental stores out of business by making mail-order distribution of DVDs possible on a global scale.

2. **Threat:** While celebrating their success, the Trojan horse of digital streaming arrives unannounced. When the company's leadership fails to recognize the need to adapt, this particular disruption almost puts them out of business.

3. **Hero comes to the rescue:** Fortunately, the CEO understands what is happening, solves the issue quickly and turns the company into not only the leading provider of mail-order movies, but also one of the largest providers of streaming movies over the internet.

4. **And they all live happily ever after:** Company then confounds all expectations when it becomes the first large non-content-producing company to trailblaze making its own blockbuster movies and TV series.

    Consumers receive inexpensive and easy access to the TV shows and movies they want, when they want them. The company's investors and millions of TV and movie fans are very happy indeed.

The setting is important in storytelling, as it frames the entire narrative. For a brand, the setting is the context in which your product exists for customers. Know what kind of territory you're entering and what your landscape looks like by carefully watching your competition.

Airbnb, for instance, not only captured consumers' hearts, but also made the narrative more compelling with stories of how carefully they negotiated with citizens, governments, and their corporate counterparts to place their brand narratives and products in new markets. Disruptive paths like Airbnb's are often riddled with roadblocks that require aligning with the very establishment that consumers believe they're working to take down, but those companies succeed by setting their own context for customers as not just a business but also a means to a better quality of life.

Airbnb disrupted its industry by making its brand story about freedom. The company helps travelers efficiently book a wide variety of places to stay in cities around the world.

Finally, I come to one of the more fun topics of disruption: the naming of companies and products. In an article published on profitguide.com on June 24, 2014, Steve Brearton describes a few approaches used for several decades to create names for disruptive and/or innovative companies, products, and services.[15] The last approach listed below was added by me because it's one of my favorite devices for naming businesses and really anything, for that matter.

1. **Misspell a word.** A misspelling of googol, the word for ten to the hundredth power, the name Google was meant to represent the impossible amount of data organized by the search company. Other firms that simply chose to misspell their names include Citi, Bawte (bought), Doweet, and Fashism.

2. **Blend words.** Claiming "the most comprehensive and swiftest name change of a global company ever done," Andersen Consulting blended "accent" and "future" to come to Accenture. Other examples include Verizon (veritas + horizon), Xstrata (extraction + strata) and Compaq (computer + pack).

3. **Add and drop letters.** Digg founder Kevin Rose chose "Dig" to signify a user's ability to dig up stories from the news aggregator.

[15] Brearton, Steve. "What's In a (Disruptive) Name?" Profitguide.com. June 24, 2014. http://www.profitguide.com/manage-grow/sales-marketing/whats-in-a-disruptive-name-66953

Dig changed to Digg when Rose found dig.com already registered as a domain name. Flickr, Tumblr, Scribd and Consumr are also well-known brands that dropped letters.

4. **Spell words backwards.** Software maker Xobni tags itself "your smarter address book," but the name is "inbox" spelled backward. "It was originally pronounced 'ZOH-bnee,'" the firm wrote on its website. Harpo Productions (Oprah Winfrey) and Serutan (Natures) used the same techniques to come up with their brands.

5. **Use a word that at first glance has no relation to anything your company does.** Although the brand names Amazon and Apple were chosen for distinct—not immediately obvious—reasons, a visitor from another planet would be very confused indeed to discover that neither company has anything to do with rivers or fruit. A name like jet.com might hint that their delivery service is as fast as a jet, but you have to look closely at their ads before you figured that out. Or is that the whole idea?

Contact us at **www.JohnFFurth.com** to learn more about how we help you and your company prepare for and execute strategies to successfully disrupt your competitors and industry.

PART EIGHT

MANAGING THE CHAOS OF BIG AND AUDACIOUS DISRUPTIONS

SECTION 33

Planning and Execution in an Uncertain Environment

You've proven that you're smart enough to come up with a potentially successful disruptive concept. Using your charisma and persuasiveness, you've convinced your family and close friends to invest enough so you can put together an enthusiastic and committed team who works feverishly over several weeks to prepare a detailed business plan and flashy charts meant to enthrall any investor who comes your way. You've even received a sizable amount of initial funding from a well-known VC fund.

Now throw the fruits of all that labor into a drawer, because your ability to make things happen has nothing to do with how well you ideate, draw Powerpoint charts, crunch numbers and tell compelling stories. That is, until your investors eventually start rattling the cage looking for updates to your plan, and you'll be required to report on how you're progressing with the financial goals, operating metrics (also known as key performance indicators, or KPIs), and action plans with clearly defined steps and accountable parties.

A great vision may remind your team and other stakeholders they are headed to a better place, short-term and medium-term plans are supposed to get them there as quickly as possible with the least amount of collateral damage. The reality is that nothing is certain. That map you and your team worked so hard to prepare couldn't possibly take into account the myriad things you just didn't know you didn't know. And let's face it, no one has learned to accurately predict the future, I don't care what the best strategists tell you.

At some point, somebody is going to ask the dreaded question: "What is your strategy?"

For help with this, I need to turn to Rita McGrath.

For most of her career as a successful and well-regarded business professor, she has wrestled with the problem of what strategy means in the Age of Disruption. McGrath argues that the concept of building a sustainable competitive advantage is no longer relevant. "Instead", she says, "organizations need to forge a new path to winning: capturing opportunities fast, exploiting them decisively, and moving on even before they are exhausted."[16]

In other words, even with the best laid plans, action steps, accountabilities, and so on, unexpected events are occurring all the time—opportunities and threats present themselves in equal measure without warning, and the possibility of being disrupted is always just around the corner.

Let's go back to the SWOT analysis example used in section sixteen.

[16] McGrath, Rita Gunther. *The End of Competitive Advantage: How to Keep Your Strategy Moving as Fast as Your Business.* Boston, MA: Harvard Business Review Press, 2013.

SWOT Analysis for Software Development Company

Strengths	Weaknesses
1. Excellent working relationship with partners 2. Hard working and highly motivated team 3. Diverse backgrounds and industry expertise 4. Great entrepreneurial culture with opportunities for individuals to grow and take on responsibility	1. Young and inexperienced management team 2. Many unstructured or nonexistent processes 3. Resource constrained (especially staff) and small margin for error 4. Little or no external marketing
Opportunities	Threats
1. Many possibilities to grow and expand business 2. Better recruitment of delivery staff using new recruiter and referrals from employees 3. Better utilization of delivery staff to improve bottom line and reduce wear and tear 4. Increased use of offshore teams	1. Potential mass exodus of delivery staff due to unhappiness and/or being overworked 2. Poor implementation and negative customer experience could possibly lead to being blacklisted by partners 3. Competition (low barriers to entry) 4. Aggressive growth without profitability

Within the context of a large, established organization, a SWOT analysis as part of a strategic review is a good way to help participants in a planning session easily grasp and discuss a lot of information. But looking at the example above, you'll immediately see limitations and weaknesses of a SWOT analysis. In fact, the one above isn't really an analysis at all. It is simply a list of high-level thoughts.

In a fast-changing, highly disruptive situation, a SWOT analysis is as good as useless the way most companies currently use it. I've therefore replaced it with a process I call OTISW—Opportunities, Threats, Ideas, Strengths, Weaknesses. While the term OTISW may lack the tidiness of the term SWOT and might not be as easy to remember, I think it reflects much more of the reality of running a disruptive company.

Opportunities and Threats: A newly formed and properly financed company needs to have the flexibility to find its footing. Although a company's business and operating model should be driven by a founder's powerful, disruptive vision, most successful disruptive companies are constantly assessing new and unplanned opportunities that could be the next big win.

Likewise, leadership teams are always assessing threats to their business from competitors, new market entrants as well as changes in technology, regulatory frameworks, etc.

Threats can also include those unexpected internal occurrences that often make our lives more miserable than a competitor eating away at our customer base. A key high-performing employee gives unexpectedly, an accident on the highway makes you late for an important meeting, a mistake on a report causes you to make a wrong judgment call, and on and on.

But buyer beware: these little annoyances often distract us from the more serious and often unforeseen bigger events that come at us like meteorites without warning and have the potential to destroy everything we've ever strived for. I'm talking about lawsuits, sudden deaths of people close to you, disruptive competitors, potentially disastrous product defects, natural catastrophes, as well as personal issues such as substance abuse and addiction.

There are thousands of leaders whose careers, businesses, or even lives end abruptly every year because they get hit unexpectedly with one of these disruptions and don't manage it well. In such situations, counterproductive behaviors can take over: the need to look good, be rational and not do something stupid, hunker down until the storm passes, etc. Though understandable, reverting to old ways of thinking and behaving could do more damage than good.

Ideas: There's a very good reason why I put a capital "I" in the middle of my SWOT process. After all, new, disruptive and innovative ideas often become the solutions to fixing many of the breakdowns—and taking advantage of great opportunities—we encounter along our personal and professional journeys.

Strengths and Weaknesses: I've always thought that putting the SW at the beginning of the SWOT analysis sent the wrong signal. It implies that when a leadership team takes stock of their business's future they always starts with the company's strength and weaknesses as if those are fixed and immutable. It's easier to pass all opportunities and threats through this fixed way of looking at the world to make decisions than doing the opposite—reevaluating and changing a company's strengths and weaknesses to fit the circumstances.

I think back on the times when I argued for change at Sony, only to be told that my ideas were "simply not part of the Sony DNA."

We know how that ended.

After all, businesses are made up of human beings and like human beings, organizations have more power to adapt their strengths and weaknesses than they give themselves credit for. Companies live and die by their ability to adapt and be agile these days. For example, what one day might appear to be a strength, such as a cost-efficient and well-oiled supply chain using web-based technologies, could become a weakness should a competitor develop a system that is entirely mobile-based, for example. And the threat could come not only from an upgrading of current technologies; a competitor could also suddenly become a threat if its supply chain achieves greater economies of scale through a series of acquisitions, or if it simply takes the time to reengineer its current process and leapfrog yours.

In short order, what you considered to be one of your core strengths has become a weakness. In fact, I would argue that you had better develop a core strength of reacting and transforming your supply chain quickly, or you might find your business in serious trouble.

SECTION 34

AGILE EXPERIMENTATION

A ccording to Techopedia, "Agile methodologies promote a project management process that encourages frequent inspection and adaptation. This leadership philosophy encourages teamwork, self-organization and accountability. [Agile Software Development] ASD is . . . a set of engineering best practices that allows for rapid delivery of high quality software."[17]

In practice, this means that large, complex software projects with many unknowns and/or a significant amount of upfront discovery can be broken down into short segments or "sprints" that take between a few days and one or two weeks to complete. If done well, agile development increases the likelihood of a project's success and the quality of the deliverables while reducing costs and time to completion.

This basic idea can also be applied to transformative disruptions when many traditional rules and practices may be challenged without knowing exactly what will replace them. I call this agile experimentation.

This approach produces some of the same outcomes as agile development and can be useful at both smaller and larger companies. Small companies—even if they are fully funded—are always resource- and time-constrained. But even the largest companies run the risk of blowing through millions, even billions of dollars and wasting a lot of time if they don't apply some principles of agile experimentation when preparing the rollout of potentially disruptive new businesses.

I've highlighted examples of two clients of mine who apply their companies' skill sets in agile development to test new disruptive ideas that could positively impact their existing companies and/or lay the basis for new, profitable business lines.

---

[17] "Definition of Agile Software Development from *Techopedia*. Accessed February 26, 2018. https://www. techopedia. com/definition/13564/agile-software-development.

Naushad is thirty years old. For the last three years he has been building and running a company that implements and customizes Salesforce software for organizations. One idea he was particularly enamored of arose out of the numerous disappointments he's faced when hiring employees who ended up being poor performers. Understandably, these problems have caused him considerable anxiety, inefficiencies, and lost opportunities. Naushad, like many entrepreneurs of his generation with disruptive ambitions, thought he had found a way to disrupt current practices and come up with something vastly better.

The idea he came up with and tested was a kind of "reverse Glassdoor." (Glassdoor is a website where employees and former employees anonymously review companies and their management.) Using this app, employers could rate employees—underperformers, top performers, and everything in-between—in a forum that was accessible to other employers, given certain permissions, etc.

On the surface, his idea passes most of the tests of a potentially successful disruptive business: Yes, this is a major issue for millions of employers. And yes, the prevailing services and products that have evolved to help employers with the conundrum of hiring don't seem optimal, given that the hiring problem still exists for so many people. There are multiple available tools, instruments, and technologies, such as the Predictive Index (PI), DiSC, Myers-Briggs, and so on, to help hiring managers better understand the kind of employees they need. There are also organizations, such as Vistage, that train people in the skills necessary to spot the right employees quickly and then hire and develop them to be the best they can be. There are also background checks, credit checks, and so forth to help with hiring decisions.

Unfortunately, Naushad soon discovered his idea didn't pass other crucial tests, and it butts up against hurdles that would require some fundamental shifts in our legal and cultural framework before they could be overcome:

1. Most states have clearly defined employment laws that make it easy for employees to sue former employers who speak badly about them and cause them not to get another job.

2. Even if that weren't the case, there are numerous reputational issues employers face if they are too vociferous in castigating a poorly performing former employee, even in a closed platform such as Naushad was thinking of. Besides which, who would want to work for a company that routinely speaks ill of the people who have previously worked there?

3. If nothing else, any good leader knows that he or she also has a major hand in how an individual employee is inspired to perform. Most businesspeople are not particularly interested in hanging out their dirty laundry for everyone to see.

But Naushad is smart, ambitious, and highly motivated. With some hard work and disruptive thinking, he might eventually come up with a solution that sidesteps many of the barriers his current idea faces. Even then, however, he will have to ask himself whether he has the intestinal fortitude to execute his idea.

Ashish—whose story you may remember from earlier—is in his late thirties. His company has been in existence for more than ten years and sells products and services for data security, web experience management, operational intelligence, web center sites, and project management. The company partners with software platforms such as Oracle, Splunk, Drupal, and others and has built a core capability of agile development. This ensures delivery of more first-rate projects, which in turn helps Ashish's company to better achieve its primary goal of forming long-term, trusting relationships with a core group of marquee clients.

The company's leaders recently used their agile skill sets to get through the process of developing an alternative to the dysfunctional system used by many corporations to buy professional services.

Purchasing departments at large companies have always been important partners in making decisions about commodities and other tangible items. But since the mid-1990s, they have also become an integral part of the decision-making process for hiring external service companies, such as high-end strategy consultants, lawyers, and software developers. These providers tend to offer services that can contribute immense value to a client's business, but whose outcomes by nature may not be entirely clear when a project plan is prepared.

The role of purchasing managers as safeguards against excess, unjustified high fees, and poor performance may be beneficial in some cases, but their involvement in choosing, negotiating, paying for, monitoring, and evaluating projects using outside service providers has also added immense complexity and inefficiencies for everyone. Not only are most service companies—from the smallest to the largest—unhappy with the current situation, but many of their clients at such companies are even more unhappy that they've lost so much control over projects key to the success of their businesses.

For several years, Ashish's company has been struggling with the fixed-project-fee model purchasing departments prefer (regardless of whether their actual clients like it). As the name implies, these projects contractually specify outcomes or deliverables, as well as budgets, before they begin.

As soon as something unforeseen occurs in a fixed-fee project, Ashish's managers have to halt work to negotiate scope changes with the client and the relevant purchasing departments. In the process, the project team loses valuable time and energy that could be better spent doing the work. As professionally as they try to handle these situations, Ashish's salespeople and project managers often also have to deal with recriminations and finger-pointing, which can potentially damage important working relationships between teams and clients.

Even when a project comes in under budget and on time, there is always the danger that a client thinks Ashish's team purposefully overpriced the engagement and/or skipped steps and delivered a lower-quality product. Often, the client—at the insistence of his or her purchasing manager—goes back and figures out how they used their rate card to price the project to try to explain the discrepancy. Unfortunately, this provides clients with yet another future tool to negotiate rates as far down as possible or to force Ashish to use cheaper but often less-qualified resources. Paradoxically, this can easily damage client-provider relationships just as badly as projects that go less well.

Ashish and I discussed alternative pricing methods, such as time-and-materials (when a consultant directly bills clients for every hour the team works) and value-based pricing (an up-front fixed fee with the possibility of a bonus if certain milestones are hit or exceeded), but he wasn't happy with any of those options.

The team wrestled with a variety of ideas for several weeks without finding a suitable solution until Ashish had his fateful encounter with an option-heavy hamburger restaurant. (See section twelve.)

Thus was born a unique "gamification" approach that uses points instead of dollars to price projects. As they refined the system, Ashish and his team decided to keep the value of the points constant regardless of the client or project, in much the same way that airlines use loyalty miles. (Interestingly, I haven't heard any ideas yet from Ashish about giving away points to increase customer loyalty.) Their first and most immediate goal was to reduce or even eliminate the need for customers to revert to the company rate card.

Once a project is scoped out and the points needed to pay for it are agreed to, the team organizes the project into agile-style sprints of between two and five days and allots points to each segment. If for some reason a sprint ends up costing more than the points allotted to it, Ashish's company "eats" the difference. At the same time, however, he makes it clear that more points might have to be allocated for the next sprint than originally planned so the situation doesn't occur again. If the sprint ultimately uses fewer points, Ashish's team might add in another feature or start the next sprint ahead of schedule so the client feels he or she is getting full value.

With this new point system in place, Ashish's team approached four of their top clients to find an opportunity to test the system. By June

2017, they had a client, a large hedge fund, willing to give this new approach a chance.

Four months later, I was talking to Ashish's lead sales person, Sandeep, about the company's sales and marketing strategy for the coming year. We started talking about how well the first project using the new point system had gone. The client was delighted that there were no significant delays, and although the project had finished slightly over budget, it was easy for Sandeep to explain the causes. More importantly, he didn't try to negotiate a payment for the extra work, instead asking that they be more generous with the points allocated to future projects. The increased level of trust and confidence generated by the experience quickly led to more requests for project proposals, which Sandeep was in the middle of happily preparing.

Sandeep's team is now able to get sign-off for an entire project instead of submitting Statements of Work (SoWs) for every agile sprint. The only thing clients have to do is buy more points if necessary, which takes just a few minutes instead of the hours usually needed to fill out paperwork and negotiate with multiple parties.

Unfortunately, at the same time, Sandeep is finding it difficult to articulate the value proposition of using points to other clients well enough to convert them to the new system—something we have earmarked to work on early in 2018.

Time will tell whether this starts a major wave of disruption to how large companies hire and utilize high-end service providers, or whether Ashish's company will be able to keep this little, but very potent, competitive advantage all to themselves.

SECTION 35

Failure, Success, and Everything In Between

y friend Al is living proof that the American rags to riches story is still a reality for many people. Although he comes from simple blue-collar roots, Al built a highly successful wealth management business servicing high net worth individuals and families around the world.

Like every ambitious entrepreneur Al survived several crises over his forty-three years in business. But each time he gave himself the permission to rethink his life's mission and the way he was running his business. He would then discard things that weren't working any longer while incorporating new ideas. Step by step Al forged a more sustainable and fulfilling path for himself and his clients, family, and friends.

In the middle of some of the darkest moments in his life, Al would meet someone who mentored him through the pain, helped him learn from it, and put him on the path of rebuilding his life and business. When you are committed to finding a way out—even if at that moment you just want to curl up and disappear—you'll always find people ready and able to help you.

Al started a certified public accountant (CPA) firm in the early 1980s, but when he found it difficult to get agreement on several issues with the other partners, he left the partnership to start another company. It wasn't going to be an accounting firm, though. On the advice of an early mentor of his, Al decided to open a wealth management company, which meant he really was starting all over again.

Things went very well until the financial meltdown in 1987. Many of his clients were heavily involved in the real estate industry and they saw their businesses and real estate holdings crumble within just a few months. Al's business and real estate investments followed suit.

In the space of a few years, he had already gone through two major disruptions to his career and company, but this time it was not a result of a personal decision; instead, the disruption came from external circumstances. This second disruption was much harder for Al to come to terms with, and it took several months before he was able to deal with the fallout in a proactive and positive way.

A new mentor helped him regroup and get back to work—an aggressive and wise businessman in Dallas who had been referred to Al by an extremely successful businessman.

For the first time in his life, Al had to come to terms with personal failure—not just any failure, but a big, messy failure that had wide-ranging consequences for himself, his family, his clients, and his staff. At some point in his conversations with his mentor in Dallas, Al learned what it meant to disrupt things he had thought were truisms about himself and business and get back into action. Once he got past that, he did something he had hoped he would never have to do: He laid off one-third of his staff.

In the process, Al discovered something else key to success—proactive conversations. By talking seriously and meaningfully with his vendors and clients, he bought the time and space he needed to replace the 25 percent of the clients he had lost.

But there was another, equally important lesson his mentor taught him. Although Al was a CPA, it was not until he decided to become a wealth advisor that he created the first financial plan for himself. Still, he had never put together a goal-oriented plan for himself or his company that required him to be accountable for achieving those goals. Once he had such a plan with a crystal-clear mission, Al found his ability to communicate to his team, clients, and others vastly improved.

Things went well until the late 1990s, when a personal crisis required him once again to make changes that would transform his life and business. He had made a lot of money by then but realized he was not happy with himself, his leadership capabilities, or his business. He and his wife didn't want the next twenty-five years of their lives to look like the previous twenty-five.

This led to a divorce and major retooling of his approach to running his company. Al had developed the bad habit of running his firm through consensus, and he could only make hard decisions after gaining everybody's input. Not only did such an approach slow the firm down, but it also suddenly became clear to Al that he had not taken the kind of responsibility he should have for running his firm. Al learned to differentiate between circumstances when a command-and-control approach versus a consensus-building approach would get the results he was looking for. Most importantly, he discovered that the true value a CEO/business owner brings to the table is to be the visionary and cultural leader. *How you show up is how your organization will be.*

Even though it scared his staff, Al ended up firing his president when he realized the extent to which the relationship with him had deteriorated beyond repair.

All of this helped Al survive the financial meltdown in 2007 and 2008 with less wear-and-tear than past crises. In the wake of those events, Al made the decision to stay small and very high-end. He hired a CIO and invested millions of dollars in upgrading his staff and putting new processes in place. He also actively discarded the traditional, goals-oriented, wealth management business model and has since transformed his firm into much more by incorporating the hard and soft skills he has acquired over the years.

Now, in addition to helping his clients build wealth through wise investments and good tax planning, Al's firm helps them build their companies properly, handle crises better, and have a life they love. His team reflects that diversity and depth of expertise—something I've never seen at other small accounting or wealth management firms, or any professional services company, for that matter.

Al has written and published an excellent book about his journey. He has found new love, a beautiful apartment in New York City and one in

Paris, and has a wide range of deep and longstanding friendships. Al feels it is important to give back and steps in to help others who reach out to him as best he can. These are gifts that several of my Vistage members and I have benefitted from with no requirements to return the favor, although we all hope to be able to do so at some point.

A lot has been written about the value of failing. There is a commonly held belief that if you don't fail, you won't learn and then succeed. But that all depends on how you define failure. For me, failure is when you are forced to stop whatever you're doing and close it down, often never returning to that particular activity or business again.

For example, during one of my conversations with Rob, I asked him point-blank how he would know his venture had been a failure if it came to that. His answer was quick and to the point—when he runs out of money. When that happens, pretty much all bets are off.

At that point, I suspect Rob will never try to build such a platform again, but will move on to something more reliable or more easily implementable. That's certainly an important life lesson as well.

For Al, failure is when a plan you had formulated or a series of decisions you made don't result in what you expected to happen. But in his version of failure, Al didn't close anything down; he simply made some momentous changes—some of them very painful and some of them life-altering—and got back into action.

What Al really was dealing with were short-term and long-term problems not so different from what many successful entrepreneurs discover when building businesses. While some problems can be very serious and threatening, it's the process of finding solutions and implementing them that ensure you don't destroy yourself or your company. Hopefully, they also make you stronger.

Al had the objectivity—or the support of a knowledgeable and sensitive third party—to learn from his failure and then move on. And one of the key learnings for Al was humility and vulnerability. Anyone who comes in contact with him today benefits very quickly from his intelligence, humanity, and innovative mindset.

We also have a terrible habit of beating ourselves up whenever we feel we've gone down the wrong road or caused ourselves to fail. The voices in our heads that reinforce the negative message that we never deserved success and what-were-we-thinking-anyway get louder and louder.

These are also the moments that remind you that you're a human being, like everyone else. You need to acknowledge that you have done great things, you are a success, and you will continue to be one. A feeling of abundance takes over and fills your body, brain, and heart with hope, and slowly but surely the negative voices that sometimes threaten to overwhelm us disappear.

SECTION 36

Wealth and Transformation

A few relevant facts and figures make it clear how the hardships, mistakes, and failures that go along with building big, audacious, disruptive businesses can often lead to incredible and unimaginable wealth for thousands of people.

Company	Market Value IPO	Market Value 5/7/2018	Annualized Return to Investors since IPO	CEO/Founder's Net Worth 2018
Amazon	$483	$776,070	41 percent	Jeff Bezos: $130,180
Tesla	$1,700	$51,400	53 percent	Elon Musk: $19,600
LinkedIn	$4,500	$26,250*	37 percent	Reid Hoffman: $6,200
Care.com	$445	$460	1 percent	Sheila Lirio Marcelo: Approx. $15

All dollar amounts are in millions.

* Value and annualized return at the time Microsoft purchased LinkedIn in late December, 2016

But the great disruptors—such as Jack Ma—are also actively doing what they can to transform the world. Ma isn't American, although he studied in the United States, and his Chinese-based company, Alibaba, was the single biggest IPO in the history of the New York Stock Exchange. Alibaba's market capitalization was $225 billion when it debuted on September 19, 2014. Later that year, the company reported revenue of $8.6 billion with net income of $3.8 billion. As of April 6, 2018, Alibaba's market capitalization was $410 billion, which represents an annual return of approximately 23 percent. Jack Ma's net worth is approximately $42 billion—not as large as some American disruptors, but certainly sizeable.

For many years, Ma has dedicated much of his steadily increasing wealth to defending the environment, but for the last seven years he's become more vociferous about the need to use great wealth to transform the world. While Alibaba may not be the most disruptive or transformative company itself, Ma sees the wealth he and his company have generated as a tool to facilitate broader transformation.

At the annual general meeting of shareholders for Alibaba.com in May 2010, Ma announced Alibaba Group would begin in 2010 to earmark 0.3 percent of annual revenue to environmental protection. But he also said that his company's "challenge is to help more people to make healthy money, 'sustainable money,' money that is not only good for themselves but also good for the society. That's the transformation we are aiming to make."[18]

But Ma also recognizes that money alone can't bring about significant transformation. The world's largest countries need to have informed trade, economic, and social policies.

In a television interview at the beginning of 2017, Ma pointed out that when the United States government blames China for any economic issues the United States is suffering, it is misguided. If America is looking to blame anyone, Ma said, it should blame itself. He said the United States has wasted over $14 trillion fighting wars over the past thirty years, rather than investing in infrastructure at home.

"The American multinational companies made millions and millions of dollars from globalization," Ma said. "The past thirty years, Cisco, Microsoft, they've made tens of millions—the profits they've made are much more than the four Chinese banks put together. But where did the money go?"[19]

"The world needs new leadership, but the new leadership is about working together," Ma also said in the same interview. "As a business person, I want the world to share the prosperity together."

I don't believe Ma was out to attack the United States. He was trying to reinforce the message that as the two most powerful nations on the planet, the United States and China need to collaborate and not bicker.

---

[18] "Jack Ma." *China Daily.* December 11, 2009. http://www.chinadaily.com.cn/m/hangzhou/e/2009-12/11/content_9164744.htm.

[19] Yarow, Jay. "Chinese Billionaire Jack Ma Says the US Wasted Trillions on Warfare Instead of Investing in Infrastructure." CNBC. January 18, 2017. https://www.cnbc.com/2017/01/18/chinese-billionaire-jack-ma-says-the-us-wasted-trillions-on-warfare-instead-of-investing-in-infrastructure.html.

In another rather provocative statement, while speaking at the Economic Club of New York in 2015, Ma said that while the Internet and its various platforms will usher in a wave of global conflict, it will not pit countries against each other. Instead, Ma sees the likes of China and the United States teaming up to defeat societal ills. "The third world war is going to happen, and this war is not between nations. In this war, we work together against the disease, the poverty, the climate change—and I believe this is our future."[20]

Indeed, Jack Ma isn't the only one committing his time and money to transforming the world. Contrary to what the popular press would like us to believe, Ma, Mark Zuckerberg, Jeff Bezos, and many others are giving back in big ways by supporting young entrepreneurs, promoting environmentalism and education, and eliminating inequality and unnecessary health risks among the needy.

I am not a disruptive businessman on the order of the men above. I hope, however, that I am a consistently good consultant and coach who uses his tools, techniques, and skills to help leaders make the best decisions possible. My journey has led me to a certain amount of wealth, although nothing along the lines of Jack Ma, Jeff Bezos, Bill Gates, or others. In my own small way, I am also trying to transform the world one step at a time.

Like many of my friends and colleagues whose stories appear in this book, it has also been a spiritual journey for me.

My new friend Rob, the erstwhile fixed-income ecosystem disruptor, has returned to Catholicism and the support system it provides for the days when more goes wrong than right. He stays in physical and mental shape with yoga and meditation. While he might talk about God, I talk about the universe and energy. And when Rob does yoga and meditates, I write, work out, and go for walks with my partner and our dog.

I believe there is a mental state that most disruptors need to achieve—one that gives them access to something more powerful, more attuned to the universe that almost preempts the negative. Western religions often

---

[20] "Jack Ma Looks to Charm the Pants off American Small Business Owners." *Shanghaiist.* June 12, 2015. http://shanghaiist.com/2015/06/12/jack_ma_charm.php.

call it living in a state of grace. Buddhists refer to it as having an abundance mentality. Whatever we call it, I believe great leaders understand and embrace this state as much as possible.

To live in a state of abundance or grace, you need to recognize a higher power than yourself—an energy, a God, a force that you give yourself over to. It means you give of yourself unstintingly while accepting the gifts the universe gives you with gratitude and thankfulness. You are strong in the knowledge that, indeed, things will work out and you will be able to generate wealth for thousands or millions of people. People in far-flung corners of the earth will have hope and improved living conditions. The world will become a better place.

Your belief in the universe's ability to shower everyone with abundance allows you to be confident in your choices, and if a leader forgets he is striving for abundance, he or she can quickly become a target of the media, politicians, legislators, employees, or investors.

Sometimes I work doubly hard to find the strength to soldier on and overcome the challenges that get between me and my goals. But inevitably, I meet an extraordinary person who teaches me an important lesson, or I see positive results from my work. And every so often, someone I don't even know says something to me that's very kind and thoughtful.

Those are the moments when I feel at one with whatever's out there in the universe and I remember to be grateful for both the gifts and the challenges I have been given.

Contact us at **www.JohnFFurth.com** to learn more about how we help you and your company prepare for and execute strategies to successfully disrupt your competitors and industry.

PART NINE

DON'T JUST STAND THERE, DISRUPT BACK!

SECTION 37

Your Business Might Be a Prime Target

L eaders and their organizations can easily form bad habits that make it virtually impossible to fulfill on any disruptive impulses they might have:

- They can get overwhelmed with the day-to-day tasks of keeping often-underresourced companies operating.

- They disregard the importance of good strategic planning, resulting in a lack of agreement internally regarding what their company is providing and how they are providing it.

- They have completely ignored other companies which have figured out better ways to fulfill on a similar value proposition.

- They may intellectually understand the principles of providing outstanding customer experiences, but don't know how to successfully translate them into products, services, or experiences and/or can't communicate the value proposition.

- They may also be too frightened by the risks and the potential for massive failure.

- They care more about improving their own lives than those of the world outside of themselves.

- They never understood the basic principles of providing value in the first place.

When a company slips into any one of these danger zones, its leadership has made itself potentially vulnerable to a disruption. We're not talking about a proactive, industry-defining disruption motivated by an informed leadership team, but rather an offensive against a company that isn't up to its game. Such a disruption will probably happen with very little prior warning because leadership at the company under siege ignored many obvious signs.

Unexpected disruptions can come from the government, a competitor, a new entrant into the market, or the company's own customers. Sometimes it's not even competitors from the same industry or companies with a remotely similar business model attacking a company, with little understanding of just how vulnerable they are.

We're accustomed to seeing mature products wiped out by new technologies and ever-shorter product life cycles. But now entire product lines—whole markets—are being created or destroyed overnight. Disrupters can come out of nowhere and instantly be everywhere.

Once launched, such disruptions are hard to fight. Companies find themselves suddenly in a defensive mode and forced to change direction, cut staff, and often either acquired by stronger companies—including the disruptive entities—or go bankrupt.

But there are many examples of companies, from the very smallest to the very largest, that are fighting back—or at least adjusting well to the new norm—and winning.

SECTION 38

LinkedIn's Challenge to the Recruitment Industry

For much of the second half of the twentieth century, men and women who were particularly adept at networking could enter the field of executive recruiting as a lucrative way to make a living with little or no financial investment. All anyone really needed was a telephone and a Rolodex. Because of the complicated logistics of distributing information about jobs and finding potential candidates, most companies had to hire an external party to help them market positions and then find and recruit qualified candidates.

Good headhunters could generate immense value for companies that had aggressive hiring plans and were in turn richly rewarded. Entrepreneurs and business builders quickly discovered the opportunity and founded what became large firms in the industry. And there was still room for small and medium-sized practitioners.

But as the saying goes, all good things must come to an end. Once the game-changing potential of the internet became clear, the disruption of the recruitment industry was in full swing.

The first major event occurred in the mid-1990s, when TMP Worldwide Advertising launched a website that would become Monster. com, the world's first electronic job board. Suddenly, anyone could post job openings, which could be viewed in minutes by hundreds of potentially interested and interesting job seekers. Granted, most of these listings were for lower and mid-level jobs, but the functionality soon started appearing on corporate, university, trade association, and a host of other websites.

As this technology spread, it didn't take long for some of the heaviest users of executive recruiting firms to conclude they could save millions of dollars if they simply hired external recruiters and brought them in-house. Sensing major shifts were occurring in their industry, many recruiters were glad to have some stability in their lives, even if it meant making less money.

But that was only the beginning. In 2003, LinkedIn opened for business. It quickly became the global marketplace of choice for employees and job seekers, from recent college graduates to seasoned executives. Within just a few years, one of the most valuable assets for executive recruiters—their highly developed Rolodexes—became a commodity.

As if that weren't enough, the great recession hit in 2008. Large recruitment firms that had merged with their competitors to form even larger companies were decimated. Small and medium-sized companies closed their doors.

I recently talked with three close friends who weathered the storm of the last eight years and emerged, if not victorious, at least still alive.

All three had started their careers elsewhere: David had been a banker in New York City, Jonathan had worked for Shell, and Jason had originally wanted to be an academic, although his father owned a recruitment firm for the IT industry. By the early 1990s they were all happy, productive headhunters. True to form, they built their businesses on relationships they had developed previously—David in banking, Jonathan in the oil and gas and consulting industries, and Jason in information and management consulting.

David had initially gone to work at the executive search firm Johnson, Smith and Knisely. This also happened to be the first firm bought by TMP in their massive rollup of small and medium-sized executive search firms meant to propel Monster.com to the forefront of search. TMP was a telemarketing company and not a search firm, and stumbled severely when, after spending hundreds of millions of dollars, it discovered that there were too many headhunters and too few clients. The "out-of-bounds" rule of not working for competitors that was strictly enforced in search propelled many excellent headhunters out of Monster.com and into the hands of rivals waiting in the wings.

David was one of those executive recruiters who left. He ended up jumping from firm to firm every two years before finally going independent in 2006. Jonathan basically disbanded his recruitment firm in 2008 and started rebuilding his business one client at a time. Jason, the youngest and most technologically savvy of the three, made a go of it with an internet-based recruiting firm that didn't quite work out, so by 2013, he had gone back out on his own.

Every now and then, one of them would think of leaving the profession or taking a job as an internal recruiter at one of their clients, but they truly love the work and couldn't imagine doing something else.

David, Jonathan, and Jason struggled to find good answers to some fundamental questions: If their most important asset, their Rolodexes, had been so devalued, then just what were their clients willing to pay to have them do? What sort of value could they deliver in the face of an industry that had been thoroughly commoditized into seamless, cheap, and (seemingly) efficient transactions?

The only good news was that they weren't alone. The bad news was, no one had an answer for them. Even their most loyal clients—often the best source for good ideas—had either jumped on the internet or internal recruiting wagon and/or negotiated their rates with my friends so aggressively as to make it impossible to do the work properly. In David's case, a lot of his clients retired.

It was true that many companies still went to external recruiters to fill either very senior positions or to find experts in extremely niche businesses, but those searches more often than not went to big, retained executive search firms.

Because my three friends' clients were professional service firms in banking and various segments within the consulting industry, they tried to see if there was something they could learn from them. They acquired a few new business development skills and learned some best practices in writing and disseminating original thought capital as marketing collateral. But optimizing how you find clients when they just weren't buying any longer didn't really mean that much in the long run.

Jonathan and Jason dabbled in contingency recruitment, i.e., getting paid only if they successfully filled a position. But those assignments were usually very difficult and unrewarding both financially and psychologically. Jonathan also considered changing his business model to one more like consulting which, with its project and deliverable-based approach, seemed on the surface to be quite similar. Unfortunately, he quickly learned that there were some fundamental differences between what makes a good consultant and what makes a good executive recruiter. Ultimately, the transition became less attractive.

During our recent discussion, the three of them were able to lay out very clearly what they had been through and where they had landed. They are still proud executive recruiters, but have found their own individual ways of adapting to the new norm. It's also helped that many of their clients have tried their own solutions, only to discover the limitations of trying to do everything themselves.

David and Jonathan have always seen themselves more as trusted advisors than executive recruiters. Jonathan in particular has a strategic and analytical way of looking at issues and is not averse to taking risks. While this mindset sometimes takes him down some rabbit holes, it also enabled him during past crises to look deeply at where he could add the most value for his clients.

He realized quickly that he could help consulting clients solve one of their most vexing problems. As difficult as it may be to find and recruit top talent, it's even harder to get newly hired partners quickly up to speed and profitable while ensuring long-term retention.

With this understanding, Jonathan likes to say he stood the recruitment model on its head. His clients may pay him to recruit good people, but Jonathan says his real clients are actually the executives he places, some of whom he's known for decades. This ensures that he puts people in jobs that make sense for them at the time, which in turn makes for better long-term commitment. He also works hard with consulting companies to find ways to integrate outside senior hires faster and more sustainably.

David and Jonathan work at the highest levels at their client organizations. They have embraced technological disruptions because these have simplified much of the transactional part of the business. David tells the story of how he got into some trouble during a search for a head of marketing for a small insurance company and turned to LinkedIn as a potential solution. To his surprise and delight, within three weeks he had unearthed fifty good candidates. Thirty days later, he successfully completed the search—something unheard of even just a few years earlier.

The youngest of the three, Jason decided years ago that the best way to compete with the larger recruiting firms was just not to. His target clients are small and medium-size consulting firms, and he services all their hiring needs, not just the upper echelons. Technology has ultimately provided him with the tools to do multiple searches for his clients faster with fewer resources and at lower cost, making his services very attractive to companies that have fewer financial resources available to them.

David, Jonathan, and Jason have now managed to get ahead of a curve that many of their clients are still trying to make sense of. Although they often have to spend a lot of time explaining why technology makes them as effective as larger recruitment firms which have thousands of recruitment staff to throw at projects, it is a pitch they are quickly refining.

Perhaps with time and some luck, they will pose the next big disruption to their bigger competitors.

SECTION 39

Walmart Takes on Amazon; Amazon Takes over Whole Foods

Despite the inroads made by Amazon during the first twenty-three years of its existence, Walmart is still the granddaddy of retailers by a wide margin. But the C-suite at Walmart is aware of how Jeff Bezos and his company are disrupting the traditional retailing model and threatening Walmart's leadership position in the long term.

Doug McMillon, who became Walmart's CEO in 2014, was determined to narrow the gap between Walmart's third-place ranking in worldwide e-commerce and Amazon's lead as the number one e-commerce site in the world.

McMillon's first big step was to purchase Jet.com for $3.3 billion in 2016 and put Jet's chief executive, Marc Lore, in charge of Walmart's overall e-commerce business.

Lore quickly introduced changes such as free two-day shipping while expanding its online assortment from eight million items at the start of 2016 to more than twenty-two million items by March 2017. (That's still just a mere fraction of the more than 300 million items Amazon has available. In fact, Walmart probably only stocks in total about two-thirds of Amazon's inventory—or approximately 200 million items—across all its retail formats.)

At the same time, Walmart said it would combine its own buying for products sold at its stores with purchases it makes for its website. Until recently, the store and online buying teams of the world's largest retailer had operated independently.

This strategy is intended to stamp out duplicate efforts. Walmart has committed itself to making the buying process more efficient for itself and its vendors and improve coordination between its buying teams. The company also intends to apply its brick-and-mortar expertise in securing the lowest possible prices to its e-commerce business. The move will help Walmart make items at its nearly 4,600 United States stores available online. Many store suppliers still don't sell online because of low sales volumes.

Just a few months after Walmart unveiled its new strategy, Amazon made a bold and far more aggressive move: it purchased Whole Foods for $13.4 billion. This took Amazon's physical presence to a new level, as the grocery chain had more than 460 stores in the United States, Canada, and Britain, and sales of $16 billion in 2016.

Walmart shot back almost immediately. On June 17, 2017, a day after the announcement of the Amazon/Whole Foods acquisition, Walmart made its its acquisition of the apparel retailer Bonobos for $310 million public. Although this transaction may be much smaller in terms of size, it's just as strategically significant to Walmart as Amazon's move is to the e-retailer.

Bonobos may have built its brand on the back of a successful online business, but it also has a chain of equally successful retail stores. Thus, the acquisition brings a unique capability to Walmart—best practices in managing two distinct channels in tandem, not separately, as has been the case for 99 percent of all retailers to date.

There's an interesting side note here: Bonobos addresses a higher-end and pricier segment—in this case, menswear—than Walmart has in the past. One could even say this acquisition potentially flies in the face of the company's mission statement: "Saving people money so they can live better." But a better way of looking at this acquisition is that in any segment Walmart sells to, whether low, middle, or high-end, it will always try to be the lowest priced.

On Monday, August 29, 2017, the first day Whole Foods opened as a subsidiary of Amazon, it announced it had lowered prices on a range of items. And because 70 percent of Whole Foods customers were also Amazon Prime customers, additional discounts became available to that large group. Amazon might have a long way to go before it is as price-competitive as Walmart, but the company knows what it has to do to fight back.

More than anything else, Amazon has an innovative and pioneering culture which means it can hire the best and brightest technology experts, engineers, lawyers, and businesspeople in the world to make things happen. The company is also willing to fight to succeed, occasionally resorting to aggressive, no-holds-barred tactics, which is really no different than most highly successful technology-driven businesses.

Although it has always had an aggressive streak, Walmart has built a folksy, polite, down-to-earth, very middle-America and conservative culture. McMillon is working hard to change that culture to take on the challenge, but it's a major undertaking for a company of that size and with such a legacy. Whatever shifts Amazon will have to make going forward, undoubtedly its pioneering culture will prove to be more adaptive and agile than Walmart's.

Amazon's innovative spirit means, for example, that if the consumer doesn't see value from the current way Amazon does business, then Bezos and company will throw out what's not working and develop something better. They have no interest in maintaining any technology or system that doesn't support their core mission of being the most customer-centric company in the world. Walmart is anything but disruptive, and their leadership's tactics are baby steps in comparison with the boldness with which Amazon is creating its future.

SECTION 40

The United States Health Care System: A Story of Disruptions and Counterdisruptions

I n a world where no company, industry, government is not witnessing disruption as never before, there is one industry that stands head and shoulders above all others for the degree it is battered daily by highly disruptive forces; at the same time, it's seemingly immune to any significant change. That industry is the United States health care system.

Undoubtedly, the energy unleashed by these dynamic forces has fostered the discovery and successful commercialization of a series of life-saving and life-enhancing products, therapies, and devices that have transformed the world. But at the same time, the United States is the only wealthy, industrialized nation that does not have a universal health care system. In 2010, the percentage of Americans without health insurance was 16.3 percent, or 49.9 million uninsured people. To add insult to injury, the share of the American economy spent on health care had increased from 7.2 percent in 1970 to 17.9 percent in 2009 and 2010.

The U.S. Healthcare Industry's Ecosystem until 1945*

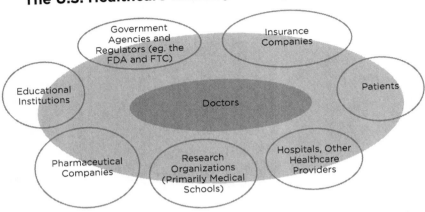

*The size of the bubble approximates the relative level of influence of other players in the marketplace.

For centuries, physicians stood at the center of the United States health care system. They were the primary decision-makers about what therapy or drug regime a patient would receive and from whom. In fact, until the late 1800s, doctors were not only dispensers of therapeutic products, but very often the developers, producers, and marketers of drugs and medical devices as well.

From 1850 to 1900, the most prominent of the current American pharmaceutical companies were founded. A unique payer/user dynamic contributed to the attractiveness of the industry for entrepreneurs, as it ensured a certain consistent level of revenue and profitability: insurance companies were expected to pay the price of whatever the doctors prescribed.

Eventually, several leaders in this burgeoning industry—especially Colonel Eli Lilly—advocated federal regulation of the pharmaceutical industry. Many of his suggested reforms were enacted into law in 1906, resulting in the creation of the Food and Drug Administration.

Thus, the foundation of our modern health care system was laid. For a while, a delicate balance among all stakeholders was maintained. While great differences in the quality of care, often based on an individual's level of income, were already a fact of life, hospitals and other providers worked diligently to provide as much care to as many citizens as possible.

The first major disruption to this system was part of American industry's general drive for democratization during the 1930s and '40s—in itself a form of disruption. The drug industry developed manufacturing processes for the sort of products that once only the wealthiest could afford, making them cost-effective and readily available for a large section of the population. In particular, penicillin was produced in large batches during wartime, dramatically lowering the cost and increasing the supply of this transformative medicine. Pharmaceutical companies began a rapid ascent in influence, power, and financial strength.

The U.S. Healthcare Industry's Ecosystem from 1945 until 2010*

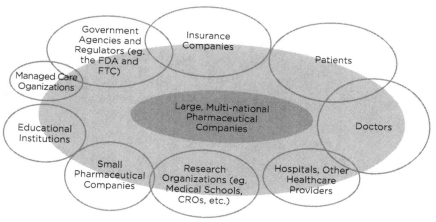

*The size of the bubble approximates the relative level of influence of other players in the marketplace.

A few of the largely privately held drug companies, such as Pfizer, went public in the 40s, which gave them access to capital to grow and consolidate. By the 1970s, large drug companies had usurped the position of doctors as the central player around which the rest of our health care system revolved.

While physicians were no longer the sole decision-makers, they still played an important role; they were still the main conduits between pharmaceutical companies and patients. And drug companies wooed them to excess with gifts, invitations to conferences, and paid education to ensure they continued to prescribe their biggest moneymakers.

But to many it was clear that the large pharmaceutical companies were walking a fine line between dramatically increasing the world's standard of living and running afoul of public opinion because they were making so much money. Regardless of that, it's hard to argue that the industry didn't understand the importance of putting the patient at the center of everything they did, and their products have transformed the world immeasurably.

But drug prices kept going up—driven by the high cost of R&D—and eventually a key series of disruptive events started in 1968, quietly and unheralded at first, but over time developing into a major force. Pharmacy benefit management companies (PBMs) were formed as a first attempt to bring drug prices down. They processed insurers' drug prescriptions, reimbursed pharmacies for those prescriptions, and maintained formularies (the list of drugs a health insurer deems medically safe). Most importantly, PBMs used their sizable patient networks to independently negotiate lower reimbursement rates with pharmacies and discounts with drug makers. Being independent meant that PBMs had an incentive to pass those savings back to their health plan sponsors, and thus, ultimately, to patients.

It's debatable just how seriously pharmaceutical companies initially took these potential disruptors to their business model. As long as the largest companies kept producing and distributing blockbuster drugs that transformed the world's health, the PBMs were careful about treading too heavily.

By the beginning of the 1990s, most of the larger drug companies had become very rich and most of them except the largest, Pfizer, had taken their eye off their pipelines. Pfizer alone was poised to release some of its most successful products ever: Zoloft, Lipitor, Norvasc,

Zithromax, Aricept, Diflucan, and Viagra. The other large pharmaceutical companies began pursuing other strategies that were not as effective. They started cutting costs, focusing their efforts away from noncore activities, and (most damagingly) trying to streamline and better manage their R&D pipelines.

A few drug companies also decided they should try to minimize the threat of the PBMs and regain some control of pricing by acquiring the largest of them. In other words, they tried to disrupt their disruptors. Merck and Medco merged in November, 1993. SmithKline Beecham then acquired Diversified Pharmaceutical Services in May 1994, followed by Eli Lilly's acquisition of PCS Health Systems in July 1994.

The officially stated reason for these mergers was to provide the acquirers with a competitive edge, building in efficiencies that would help the companies keep up with the demand for better health care at lower prices. Indeed, the alliances provided drug companies with phenomenal access to data and shifted their focus to ways of promoting long-term health.

But many people also recognized that a PBM owned by a pharmaceutical company posed a potential conflict of interest. A PBM could very easily promote just the parent company's products to the detriment of its competitors, and not always in the best interests of some patients. It wasn't long before the Federal Trade Commission (FTC) challenged Eli Lilly's acquisition of PCS, alleging violation of the antitrust laws. In addition, the Commission pledged to monitor the industry carefully and cautioned that it might take future action if it concluded there were signs of anticompetitive conduct in the industry.

In 1998, the FTC announced an agreement with Merck and Co., Inc. resolving antitrust concerns resulting from Merck's acquisition of Medco. The commission alleged that Merck's acquisition of Medco, a pharmacy benefits manager, had substantially lessened competition in the manufacture and sale of pharmaceuticals and in the provision of PBM services, leading to higher prices and reduced quality.

The settlement required Medco to take steps to diminish the effects of any unwarranted preference that might be given to Merck's drugs over those of Merck's competitors in connection with the pharmacy benefit management services that it provides.

In addition to the FTC's warnings, consumers and private employers had sued Medco, Express Scripts Inc., and AdvancePCS, alleging double-dealing. Suits claimed they included expensive drugs on their lists of preferred medicines for their own benefit rather than the benefit of their clients. The company was also accused of promoting use of Merck's own drugs, including expensive cholesterol fighter Zocor, rather than less-expensive drugs—a potential conflict of interest that analysts cautioned could trigger antitrust concerns.

In 1998, Eli Lilly responded by selling its PCS unit to Rite Aid Pharmacy, and in 2003 Merck spun off its Medco division to its shareholders.

By sticking to its most powerful strategy—producing disruptive and transformative drugs—Pfizer spent most of the 1990s vastly outperforming their competitors. The company also managed to avoid the kind of controversy that other large drug makers attracted with their less-than-perfect strategies.

Eventually, however, even Pfizer started getting mired in many of the same problems their competitors had run into during the decade before. By 2016 the company had embarked on a series of questionable strategies to keep shareholders happy—they simply raised prices between 5 percent and 20 percent for 100 of their biggest moneymakers.

But the winds of change that the PBMs had started began to blow even more heavily in the late 1980s as political leaders seized on the opportunity to be seen as the savior of an increasingly dysfunctional system. It bubbled and boiled until the then first lady Hillary Clinton famously threw her hat into the ring. Her lead was eventually taken over by President Obama and Nancy Pelosi in 2010, when they finally passed the Affordable Care Act.

The U.S. Healthcare Industry's Ecosystem after the passing of the Affordable Care Act in 2010*

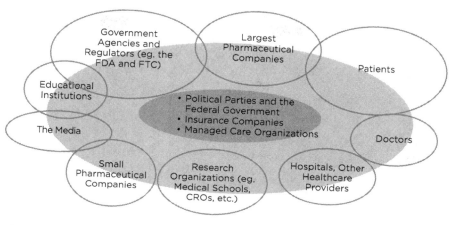

*The size of the bubble approximates the relative level of influence of other players in the marketplace.

Thanks to the Affordable Care Act of 2010, the growth in health care expenditure as a percentage of gross domestic product has been halted. It even declined somewhat, from 17.9 percent to 17.5 percent. More importantly, an estimated twenty million people gained health insurance coverage between the passage of the health reform law in 2010 and early 2016, according to United States Health and Human Services. This includes millions of people who received private health insurance on the Affordable Care Act exchanges, those who gained Medicaid coverage under state expansion, and young adults who were able to stay on their parents' health plans until age twenty-six.

Meanwhile, the disruption in the role of the all-prescribing, all-knowing gods in white, our doctors, has continued as they find it harder to maintain private practices. Hospital ownership of physician practices jumped 86 percent between 2012 and 2015, according to a study from Avalere Health.[21] Nearly 40 percent of the nation's physicians,

[21] Young, Joanna. "Avalere White Paper: Hospital Acquisitions of Physician Practices and the 340B Program." *Avalere.* June 8, 2015. http://avalere.com/expertise/life-sciences/insights/avalere-white-paper-hospital-acquisitions-of-physician-practices-and-the-34.

or 140,000 providers, were hospital-employed, the study found. This marks a nearly 50 percent increase in hospital employment since 2012, when 95,000 physicians were employed across the country.

The system is complex, to say the least. But as long as most organizations within the health care ecosystem put consumers and patients at the center of their activities, the power of this most transformational of industries will continue unabated. More affordable services and products will be available when and where customers and consumers want them without diminishing the possibility of creating wealth for the hardworking employees, entrepreneurs, and leaders at all junctures of the system.

SECTION 41

The Journey Continues

The disruption to their industry started by LinkedIn is by no means over for my executive recruiter friends. Businessmen like Joe Meyer—who built HopStop into a major location-based app which he sold to Apple—and Jeff Nussbaum are part of the next wave of entrepreneurs intent on disrupting the recruitment industry again.

After Meyer left Apple, he began thinking about the next business he wanted to commit to. He took a hard look at the recruitment industry. Joe realized that even with LinkedIn, the current model still helps recruiters more than their client organizations and the executives they were hired to recruit.

His goal is to put the job seeker at the center of an ecosystem that would further break down the barriers between companies looking for talent and those looking for the next good opportunity. Joe sees little room for traditional recruiters and delights in the fact that executives at some of the major recruiting firms have demanded that he stop doing what he's doing.

His platform is called ExecThread, and it is the only marketplace in existence I know of that allows C-suite executives as well as managers to look for positions while letting them post any jobs they have run across in which they are not interested. This also includes positions being handled exclusively by senior executive recruiters which would never see the light of day and/or find such a large audience so quickly.

Jeff Nussbaum, on the other hand, has run staffing and recruitment organizations his entire life and had the wise forethought to have his company acquire the URL "recruit.com" at the end of the 1990s. It's only recently, however, that he found an idea he can commit to that he feels does justice to that domain name.

The basis of his business is the understanding that resumés, for most people, aren't what get them jobs. Most hiring managers have a fixed idea of the person and experience they are looking for, and sadly, most resumes never seem to fit their ideal. There are always many candidates who don't pass the first stage, and who might have been perfect for the job, but for some reason couldn't convey that properly in their resume.

What if, Jeff reasons, you could record a video of yourself talking about your job, what you love about it, and the challenges you face as well as what you'd like to do next? And what if that video was properly curated on a closed site that only allows hiring parties—and not your current employer—to view your video? Wouldn't that make more sense and do away with a lot of the effort and money involved in poring through resumes, only to be disappointed when the process takes two or three times longer than expected?

This model reverses the current approach, placing the most important part of the hiring process upfront—hearing and seeing a person talk and explain what they are looking for. That does away with the hiring company's need to slave endlessly over resumes that often just end up in the trash bin. In the age when videos are the primary mode for conveying information, Jeff's approach is more modern and less exhausting for all those involved in the early stages of the hiring process and will hopefully be more efficient and effective.

As for the initial disruptive punches thrown at each other by Amazon and Walmart over the past few years, these are nothing compared to bigger and nastier brawls looming on the horizon.

With revenues of $178 billion in 2017, Amazon still has a lot of mergers and other big, bold moves before the company comes anywhere near Walmart's 2017 revenue of $486 billion. But given Amazon's culture and the company's average annual growth rate of 17 percent over the past five years compared to Walmart's paltry 1 percent, Bezos and team might very handily achieve that goal by 2027.

Although the story in this part focuses on the battle between Amazon and Walmart, the real war is with Alibaba. Not only did the company have the highest valuation of any IPO in the history of the New York Stock Exchange, it also quickly became the largest retailer in the world in April, 2016 when it posted higher annual revenues than Walmart.

Likewise, the ongoing disruption and counter-disruption of the U.S. Healthcare system is far from over. Donald Trump and the GOP are trying to leave their mark as well—most recently by starting a process to place controls on the price of drugs, yet another attempt to disrupt the pharmaceutical industry.

Similar to not-for-profits and religious institutions, governments are mission-based and therefore adhere to different rules of engagement than businesses. In the United States, at least, the federal government is subject to a series of checks and balances that ensure no single person or entity can ever have complete and utter control. Even the President of the United States has far less freedom to act than the average CEO— something President Donald J. Trump quickly discovered. Many people therefore find the comparative slowness of our federal government's decision-making process confounding, and often the outcomes are less than we have come to expect from most large corporations. This also makes the deployment of the more aggressive disruptive techniques used in business that much more difficult.

That said, much the same way shareholders and other interested parties monitor the performance of a given business, there are KPIs to track the relative success of our federal agencies in ensuring our safety, health, financial security, and competitiveness relative to other countries. Unfortunately, these metrics can prove to be annoyingly inconclusive. There is rarely, if ever, broad consensus regarding the right plan or strategy to improve indicators that are headed in the wrong direction. Much the same thing can be said about our state and local governments which often (should) have more direct influence over our daily lives.

Our federal, state, and municipal governments do have a kind of disruption built into them—regular elections for top officials. Given the hysteria and end-of-the-world pronouncements that accompany those moments when a party (re)gains full control over the Presidency, Congress and/or Senate, it is easy to see how they conform at least to one of the definitions of a disruption. There are indeed winners and losers in the game.

At least in my lifetime, the United States health care system has proven itself impervious to any significant disruption that would simplify it, increase transparency, lower costs, and provide universal coverage without any loss in quality or service.

That is, until January 30, 2018, when none other than Jeff Bezos and two friends waded into the swamp with the hope of fixing it. That's the day Amazon announced that it would work with JP Morgan Chase and Berkshire Hathaway on disruptive solutions that would hopefully transform the American health care system.

At the time of the writing of this book not a lot of detail had yet been provided. However, I believe that they have a better chance of succeeding than the government and the thousands of entrepreneurs and business leaders that have tried before them, for the following reasons:

1. **The timing couldn't be better.** More than the gun debate, income inequality, failing infrastructure, or a myriad of other current domestic concerns, our health care system has been the number one hottest unresolved issue in the country for decades. It touches every citizen, regardless of race, level of education and income, age, or political persuasion. It not only involves our pocketbooks, but also our deepest-held beliefs and emotions about life and death. Unfortunately, our government has proven itself incapable of developing and implementing a better system.

2. **The combined financial resources and purchasing power of the partners are immense.** The combined market capitalization of Amazon, Berkshire Hathaway, and JP Morgan Chase on May 7, 2018 was $1.635 trillion. Although that's less than half the market capitalization for the entire U.S. health care industry—estimated to be $4.97 trillion—it's still more than twice the market capitalization of $720 million of the three largest

pharmaceutical companies in the world (Johnson & Johnson, Pfizer and Novartis). That's a very large war chest indeed.

3. **Three of the greatest businessmen today—Jeff Bezos, Jamie Dimon, and Warren Buffett—are committed to fixing the problem.** These men have proven time and time again that they can provide significant returns to their investors while growing their companies consistently, year after year. Their experience and skill sets are highly complementary: Bezos is the disruptive technologist and entrepreneur, Buffet is the prudent and wise investor, and Dimon is the pragmatic realist. They know that a combination of well-deployed technology, smart business models, and proper controls will win the game.

4. **They're starting their journey at home.** While the initial announcement might have rocked the global stock markets and sent shivers down the spines of many incumbents, it appears that the three partners will initially only focus on improving the quality and lowering the costs of health care for their combined 1.1 million employees. This gives them a lot of leeway to learn, experiment (within reason), and refine highly disruptive solutions before bringing them to market.

5. **There are potentially few or no conflicts of interest.** JP Morgan Chase is a banker to many of the major incumbents in the health care industry, and Berkshire Hathaway may own stock in several of the large drug companies, but none of the partners have any history operating a health-care-related business. Focusing initially only on their employees also allows them to work out of sight of competitors, legislators, and the media, which can easily put a stop to any disruption before it can get started.

6. **Other major corporations are following their lead.** Following on the heels of the Amazon-JP Morgan Chase-Berkshire

Hathaway announcement, Apple also announced it would be opening health clinics for Apple employees and their families called AC Wellness. This is a significant development, especially since Apple's operating system is HIPAA compliant. This will make it that much easier to roll out mobile applications to a wide audience when the time comes.

It's always risky to end a book with something that reads like a prediction. There's always the possibility that I will be proven wrong and there will be no way for me to hide it.

But I'm sure I'll be at least a little right, because I know the unstoppable force of disruption will continue moving mankind forward, transforming lives and forcing positive change, especially among those who resist it the most.

Every one of us has to decide whether we want to live a life of abundance, success and happiness or one of strife, poverty and illness. Because in the end, the most important lesson we can learn from the greatest disruptive leaders in the world is that no one owns your tomorrow except you.

That's something I *will* bet on.

How exposed is your organization to being disrupted? Contact us at **www.JohnFFurth.com/diagnostics** to discuss how we help organizations not only protect themselves but become more of a disruptive force than a potential disruptee.

ACKNOWLEDGMENTS

The Vistage community has provided me with valuable lessons and learnings, many of which appear in this book. More importantly, the members of my group are a daily source of inspiration and happiness. I owe them my deepest thanks and gratitude, especially to those whose stories are included in this book: Alex, Salomon, Sean, Alan, Ashish, and Naushad.

It takes a lot for businesspeople to open up to someone they barely know and talk about their personal and professional journeys. The accomplished men who allowed their stories to appear here, such as Al, Rob, Dov, Jonathan, Jason, David, Jeff, Benjamin, and Joe gave me the kind of insights and stories that added depth and relevance to my narrative.

Without the guidance and experience of Henry DeVries, my writing coach and mentor, I'd probably still be staring at my computer screen trying to figure out where to start.

Finally, I want to thank the two beings on this planet I love more than anything else—my partner Curtis and our dog, Bella. Writing your first book is not the easiest thing to do, but going through it as a bystander for a year and a half must have been even harder. I thank them for their love, patience, and support.

ABOUT THE AUTHOR

John Furth works with CEOs and their senior executives to develop cutting-edge leadership skills, plan and implement innovative business models, products and services while helping them increase the performance of their organizations.

He has spoken at the Harvard Club of New York City, the Waseda Marketing Forum in Tokyo, the National Press Club in Washington D.C., IBM's Global Innovation Outlook, National Public Radio, and in front of various trade groups and has been extensively quoted in publications such as *The Wall Street Journal, Financial Times, American Banker, Bloomberg BusinessWeek,* and *Industry Standard.* John's online column for the *New York Daily News* and his blogs on topics relating to leadership such as "Celebrating Independence: Learning When to Let Go," "Today's Virtual Leaders," and "Strategy and the Effective Leader," have attracted a wide following.

John has spent the past twenty-five years as an external and internal consultant, holding senior positions as the head of strategy groups at Hitachi Consulting, Discovery Communications, Sony Corporation, and Roland Berger Strategy Consultants. While he was the President and CEO of the Association of Management Consulting Firms (AMCF), he had the great honor of presenting a lifetime achievement to Clayton Christensen, a key moment in his decision to become an expert in disruption. Michael Raynor, an important writing partner of Clayton's, was also a frequent speaker at AMCF events.

In 2015, John became Vistage's Chair for Brooklyn, New York, a role which allows him to draw on his experience and extensive network to coach and advise CEOs and business owners of NYC-based small and medium-sized companies.

Owning Tomorrow: The Unstoppable Force of Disruptive Leadership is John's first book.

Contact Information

John F. Furth
President
Furth & Associates, LLC
365 Bridge Street, 15F
Brooklyn, NY 11201

917.626.0065 Direct

www.JohnFFurth.com

WORKS CITED

Amigobulls. "Whole Foods Market Revenue, Profits - WFM Annual Income Statement." August 28, 2017. https://amigobulls.com/stocks/WFM/income-statement/annual

Brearton, Steve. "What's In a (Disruptive) Name?" Profitguide.com. June 24, 2014. http://www.profitguide.com/manage-grow/sales-marketing/whats-in-a-disruptive-name-66953

China Daily. "Jack Ma." December 11, 2009. http://www.chinadaily.com.cn/m/hangzhou/e/2009-12/11/content_9164744.htm.

Clarke, Katherine. "Huge NYC Brokerage under Attack from a Start-up: Suit." New York Daily News. March 23, 2015. http://www.nydailynews.com/life-style/real-estate/nyc-largest-brokerage-attack-start-up-suit-article-1.2159866.

Copeland, Michael V. "Reed Hastings: Leader of the Pack." Fortune. November 18, 2010. http://fortune.com/2010/11/18/reed-hastings-leader-of-the-pack/.

DeBord, Matthew. "Why Elon Musk isn't 'deeply flawed' in his personality." Business Insider. December 11, 2015. http://www.businessinsider.com/why-elon-musk-isnt-deeply-flawed-in-his-personality-2015-12

Definition of Agile Software Development from Techopedia. Accessed February 26, 2018. https://www.techopedia.com/definition/13564/agile-software-development.

Fiegerman, Seth. "Walmart buying Jet.com for $3.3 billion to take on Amazon." CNNtech. August 8, 2016. http://money.cnn.com/2016/08/08/technology/walmart-jet-deal-amazon/index.html

Gerstner, Louis V. *Who Says Elephants Can't Dance? Leading a Great Enterprise through Dramatic Change*. New York, NY: HarperBusiness, 2003.

Krasny, Jill. "The Jeff Bezos Recipe for Disruption." *Inc.com*. October 15, 2013. https://www.inc.com/krasny/jeff-bezos-recipe-for-disruption.html.

McGrath, Rita Gunther. *The End of Competitive Advantage: How to Keep Your Strategy Moving as Fast as Your Business*. Boston, MA: Harvard Business Review Press, 2013.

Moore, James F. *The Death of Competition: Leadership and Strategy in the Age of Business Ecosystems*. HarperBusiness, 1997.

Moschella, David. "50 for 50 – The Most Important IT Disruptors of the Last Half Century." *Leading Edge Forum*. June 30, 2014. https://leadingedgeforum.com/publication/50-for-50-the-most-important-it-disruptors-of-the-lasthalf-century-2379/.

Park, Andrew. "What You Don't Know About Dell." *Bloomberg.com*. November 03, 2003. https://www.bloomberg.com/news/articles/2003-11-02/what-you-dont-know-about-dell.

Rusli, Evelyn M. "A King of Connections Is Tech's Go-To Guy." *The New York Times*. November 05, 2011. http://www.nytimes.com/2011/11/06/business/reid-hoffman-of-linkedin-has-become-the-go-to-guy-of-tech.html.

Shanghaiist. "Jack Ma Looks to Charm the Pants off American Small Business Owners." June 12, 2015. http://shanghaiist.com/2015/06/12/jack_ma_charm.php.

Statista-The Statistics Portal. "Number of stores of Whole Foods Market worldwide from 2008 to 2017." November, 2017. https://www.statista.com/statistics/258682/whole-foods-markets-number-of-stores-worldwide/

Streitfeld, David, and Christine Haughney. "Expecting the Unexpected From Jeff Bezos." *The New York Times.* August 17, 2013. http://www.nytimes.com/2013/08/18/business/expecting-the-unexpected-from-jeff-bezos.html.

Wingfield, Nick and Michael J. de la Merced. "Amazon to Buy Whole Foods for $13.4 Billion." *The New York Times,* June 16, 2017. https://www.nytimes.com/2017/06/16/business/dealbook/amazon-whole-foods.html

Yarow, Jay. "Chinese Billionaire Jack Ma Says the US Wasted Trillions on Warfare Instead of Investing in Infrastructure." *CNBC.* January 18, 2017. https://www.cnbc.com/2017/01/18/chinese-billionaire-jack-ma-says-the-us-wasted-trillions-on-warfare-instead-of-investing-in-infrastructure.html.

Young, Joanna. "Avalere White Paper: Hospital Acquisitions of Physician Practices and the 340B Program." *Avalere.* June 8, 2015. http://avalere.com/expertise/life-sciences/insights/avalere-white-paper-hospital-acquisitions-of-physician-practices-and-the-34.

Made in the USA
San Bernardino, CA
23 September 2018